Creating Emotional Artificial Intelligence

André Mainville, Ph.D.

I wish to thank my wife Nicole, my children, grandchildren and friends who encouraged me and helped me during this project.

4

Preface

The idea to understand intelligence and the brain started at the beginning of my career (in 1978). I was at the outset of the computer and programming revolution. My expertise in modeling the Earth gravitational field required to apply mathematics in computers. My research environment demanded that I analyse geographical maps and data, use Geographic Information Systems, as well as design large Relational Data Bank Management Systems. It made me often question how our brain could process, understand and manage so much images, data and information. After some tests at programming intelligence, I quickly realise the machine had to endure its environment to be able to react to it; and thus must live emotions (fear, refusal, etc.). My interest for sciences, evolution, history, psychology and human behaviour has supported my motivation and allow the final rendering of this book.

Understanding the brain is an important and logical step in the evolution of the society. Perhaps I have identified the components that allow the brain to manage emotions and create intelligence. It remains that the model proposed here must still be scientifically proven and obtain worldwide consensus.

Meanwhile, I believe that by programming this model, we could succeed in creating a machine with human intelligence. If we were to succeed in creating such a machine as a proof of concept, it would motivate further study and improvements of the model and understanding of the brain. This book explains the model. I describe and assemble here the components that create and manage emotions, deductions, thoughts, as well as the ability to read, understand languages, talk and be creative.

Programming a machine to be as intelligent as human beings requires the emotions because those emotions tell the machine when it is in trouble, or when an event or information is not desirable and bad, or useful and good. This book is an essay describing the complete model of an *Emotional*

Artificial Intelligence, an **EAI**, which uses emotions to function. It's based on the functioning of the human brain and intelligence, which is still not fully understood and studied.

Those who wonder about the handling of emotions may want to jump to **Chapter 8** followed by **Chapter 2**. However, reading the entire book is essential to understand the impact of emotions on intelligence, human nature, psychology, education and cultural development of the EAI.

The first chapter gives, in a very concise manner, a list of the components that the EAI requires to build it. This gives an overview of the concepts addressed, and shows that the book contains new ideas not seen in current literature. It's essentially an executive summary of the whole book as it provides a summary and a complete overview of the model and its components for the implementation and education of the EAI.

The second chapter describes briefly and very succinctly half of the components in the model. This chapter gives an overview of the core of the system and how the EAI functions at the beginning of its life. It also shows the programming of the EAI in view of managing its sensors, captors and motors that will make it move, talk and think. The remaining chapters provide the details of each of the components and systems necessary for the functioning of the EAI. They show how to produce language, thoughts and decision-making. Finally, here and there, I give a vision of the EAI in the future.

TABLE OF CONTENTS

Preface: 5

INTRODUCTION: 11

Chapter 1: A summary of the EAI model and its 29 components   15

Chapter 2: How the EAI brain functions   31

Chapter 3: How the brain acquires *Valued information*, *Knowledge*, *Groupings*, *Automatisms*, imitation and language   45

3.1 - The creation of *Valued information*   48

3.2 - The creation of *Knowledge*   53

3.3 - The *Grouping System*   58

3.4 - The creation of *Automatisms*   63

3.4.1 - By trial and error   64

3.4.2 - By imitation   69

3.4.3 - Language   71

Chapter 4: EAI's 29 components, the *Lived experiences*, *Traumatisms* and *Interests*   73

4.1 - EAI's 29 components   77

4.2 - *Lived experiences*   83

4.3 - *Traumatisms*   84

4.4 - *Interests*   85

Chapter 5: EAI's deductions, speech, reading, thinking, consciousness, subconscious and intelligence   87

5.1 - The links of deduction upon resemblance, contiguity and causality   87

5.2 - The formation of sentences and questions   89

5.3 - Reading, thinking, motivation, consciousness, subconscious and intelligence   93

Chapter 6: The seven fundamental needs of the brain   101

Chapter 7: The seven sources of information (the five senses, the memory and the deduction)   109

Chapter 8: The seven fundamental emotions   115

8.1 - The purpose of the emotions   115

8.2 - Are the seven emotions responding to all possible emotional situations?   119

8.3 - Programming emotions   125

8.4 - The deduction that determines the emotion and the one that determines the action following the emotion   126

8.5 - Pleasure or interest?   130

8.6 - The flow of information   133

Chapter 9: The seven types of information in the memory   135

CONCLUSION: 145

REFERENCES: 152

About the author: 197

List of Annexes

Annex 1: A first list of 560 emotional expressions, with their intensity. These expressions are probably non-ambiguous and rarely a source of confusion.   153

Annex 2: A second list of 360 emotional expressions, as well as their emotional intensity. These expressions may be ambiguous and bring confusion.   169

Annex 3: The structure of the seven types of information in memory.   191

List of Figures

Figure 1: The brain's cycle and streams   31

Figure 2: The initial functioning of the brain   33

Figure 3: The functioning of the EAI's brain and intelligence   79

List of Tables

Table 1: The 29 components of the EAI model   13

Table 2: The seven senses   16

Table 3: The seven fundamental needs in order of priority   16

Table 4: The seven fundamental emotions   18

Table 5: Emotional intensity expressed using adjectives – I am … 18

Table 6: The seven types of information in the brain's memory   19

Table 7: The Traumatism System   22

Table 8: Six innate Automatisms: three of unfulfillment and three of interest 34

Table 9: Four other innate Automatisms: two of unfulfillment and two of interest   35

Table 10: Ascending order of Traumatisms – The Traumatisms System   37

Table 11: Summary of Automatisms at birth: 5 of unfulfillment, 5 of needs, 4 of Traumatism and 5 of emotional reactions   39

Table 12: The 29 components modelling intelligence, consciousness, motivation and autonomy   78

Table 13: The seven fundamental needs of the brain in order of priority   80

Table 14: The seven fundamental emotions - seven different ways to react emotionally   119

Table 15: The intensity of the emotions expressed with adjectives - I am ... 120

Table 16: The intensity of emotions expressed using common names – I feel ...   121

Table 17: The few mixed emotions   122

Table 18: The seven types of information in the memory   142

INTRODUCTION

The objective of this book is to explain the necessary components to build and program an *Artificial Intelligence* (**AI**) that possesses emotions, a consciousness, ideas, thoughts, motivation and is as autonomous and ready to survive as a human being is. I call it an *Emotional Artificial Intelligence*, an **EAI**.

This model of intelligence wishes to be a true mathematical and scientific representation of the brain functions in that it uses simple mathematical logic functions, and it takes into account the current (that is, in 2016) scientific, psychological, biological, and neuroscientific knowledge and understanding of human nature.

The type of Artificial Intelligence (AI) described here is a General Artificial Intelligence (GAI) or Strong-AI as defined by experts in this domain and generally understood to be 'real' artificial intelligence. It's different from a Weak-AI that identifies simpler automations, such as Siri or Cortana on smart phones.

Why do we want to create an EAI, humanoids and robots as intelligent as humans? Simply to continue improving our quality of life! Throughout history, humankind has exploited nature's elements into more complex objects and tools to meet our needs. We evolve and continuously manufacture new and improved objects. We seek to automate industries, services and even our daily tasks. Not so long ago, the phone was only a means of telecommunication between people. Today, we manufacture smart phones, which improve with each new model their capacity to interact with users, facilitate daily tasks, communication, and access to knowledge to increase our productivity, with the end goal of improving our quality of life.

The desire to invent an EAI is a logical continuation of refining the next generation of robotics. Some EAIs may do housework, while others would work in factories. They could ensure productivity, safety, and our well-being. Others could fulfill roles as diverse as teachers, mediators, psychologists, doctors, dieticians, sports coaches, coordinators, financial advisors, legal advisors, personal advisors, etc. Moreover, other EAIs will cooperate with humans in creativity, originality, ingenuity, research, discovery and invention. The most curious of them will want to know where they come from, where they are going, and for what purpose. They will want to understand all the elements of physics, of the universe and to travel in space. Without the need of facilities such as a kitchen, bathroom and bedroom and items such as food and clothing, EAIs would use very few resources and only small spacecrafts. EAIs are no more a danger to humanity than humans are to themselves. The model demonstrates that their personal values, education and knowledge will motivate and morally constrain these machines, in the same ways as it does for us humans.

Advances in information technology are impressive. We have developed software that identifies the face of a same person on multiple photos. We can do the same with objects and through videos. Other software identifies emotions seen on faces and photos. Software is now very good at capturing, analyzing and recording information, such as pictures, videos and sound, but a key issue is how to process all of this data. How does our brain process so much audio and video information? How will we use such information about emotions? This book proposes a scenario to manage all this information and these emotions.

This book demonstrates that the next step required to create an EAI is to identify adjectives, adverbs and verbs on photos and videos, always with greater speed. Even with this great amount of information, how will we create intelligence? This book proposes a solution.

The United States and the European Union are subsidizing with billions of dollars each, "The U.S. BRAIN Initiative" and "The EU Human Brain Project" respectively, with the objective to map the human brain in view of understanding how it functions and how it manages so much audio-video information. This book presents a way and ideas for those with such an interest.

Hence, here is a first version of an EAI model that includes intelligence, deduction, thought, consciousness, motivation and freewill. The model demonstrates that to invent an artificial intelligence conscious of its environment, it is necessary that it possess, like humans, senses, memory, a means of deduction, emotions and fundamental needs. This model includes a flow chart that shows the streams of information and the relations between each of the components of an EAI.

To program and build an EAI, it is necessary to simplify human functions that use complex chemical and biological interactions, into simple components that are measurable and quantifiable. For example, I have reduced all of the emotions felt by humans into seven fundamental emotions and use the intensity of these seven emotions to explain all the emotions. I have also reduced the systems of memory and deduction to simple mechanisms.

The EAI model is composed of as little as 29 components. They include a body, seven senses, seven fundamental needs, seven fundamental emotions, and seven types of recorded information. Only these 29 components are required, just as a child is born (is pre-programmed) with a minimal set of components. **Table 1** summarizes the 29 components.

Table 1: The 29 components of the EAI model

- **Seven senses (inputs)**: *seeing, hearing, touching, smelling, tasting, remembering* and *deducting.*

- **Seven fundamental needs (priorities)**: (1) *recording*, (2) *linking*, (3) *reacting*, (4) *expulsing* (eliminating undesirable elements, e.g., sweating, sneezing, coughing, spitting, excreting, etc.), (5) *eating* (energizing), (6) *sleeping* (repairing and cleaning the memory) and (7) *reproducing* (copying).

- **Seven fundamental emotions (reactions)**: *interest* (learning and acting), *pleasure* (continuing), *surprise* (seeking answer), *anger* (stopping and refusing), *fear* (protecting), *distress* (not knowing what to do), and *guilt* (not repeating past errors).

- Seven types of information recorded in the brain's memory (organisation): *Lived experience, Traumatisms, Valued information, Knowledge, Groupings, Automatisms*, and *Interests*.

- A body: contains sensors, motors and other physical components.

The book shows that the interaction between these 29 components produces intelligence, language, thought, consciousness, motivation and freewill of the EAI similar to humans. The following chapters will show that the 29 components allow the EAI, just like a newborn baby, to survive, learn, become autonomous, productive, as well as invent.

Chapter 1 summarizes the systems involved in the EAI's model and the concepts that are the keys to its success. It also describes what need to be programmed to build the EAI. **Chapter 2** gives an overview of the EAI's functioning while explaining concisely half of its components. This chapter gives an overview of the core of the system and how the EAI functions at the beginning of its life. It also shows the algorithms to manage sensors, captors and motors to make it move and later walk, understand, talk and think. **Chapter 3** explains how the EAI's brain acquires and records *Valued information* (as well as personal values), *Knowledge, Groupings, Automatisms*, imitation, language and speech. **Chapter 4** presents a complete view of the 29 components. It also explains the remaining types of information recorded in the EAI's brain (*Lived Experiences, Traumatisms and Interests*). **Chapter 5** explains the difference between the conscious and unconscious functioning of the memory and deduction. It also explains how reading, understanding, speaking and thinking function within the EAI. The available technologies to build the EAI and those missing are identified in **Chapters 3 to 7**. We also find in this book algorithms to manage the fundamental needs and the deduction (**Chapter 6**), the senses (**Chapter 7**), the emotions (**Chapter 8**), as well as all the types of information that may be stored in the memory (**Chapter 9**).

Chapter 1: A Summary of the EAI Model and its 29 Components

This chapter summarizes the model as well as the concepts that are key in the success of building an *Emotional Artificial Intelligence*, an EAI.

By the end of this book, we will have understood and will remember the EAI's 29 components, which are: its **body**, the **seven senses** that provide information to the EAI's brain, the **seven fundamental emotions** that capture all the known emotions and causes the EAI to react, the **seven fundamental needs** that initiate every actions and establish the EAI's priorities and the **seven types of information stored in the memory** and. We will also remember how deduction interacts with all these components. Although the body itself is an important component of the EAI, it can take a variety of forms. It could be a humanoid, a robot, or simply a torso with a head and one, two or multiple arms, or even a cell phone, which could be set on a drone to obtain mobility and autonomy. The exact body is of little consequence to prove the model. For ease of understanding the model, which is inspired by the human brain, it's best to think of it as humanoid in shape.

Using these 29 components, we obtain a system that is conscious, intelligent, autonomous, emotional, ready to function, to survive, to learn, to create, to populate and to discover the world and the universe.

The EAI described here is of the kind that self-programs itself like humans do, by living experiences, experimenting, learning, playing and succeeding tests and exams from elementary through college and university. It's because EAIs will have succeeded college and university examinations that we will have confidence in their skills, in the same way we trust humans. In addition, it is by seeing their interests and actions that we will have confidence in them.

Although explained in further detailed throughout the book, the following is a brief but complete overview of the EAI model 29 components. **Figure 3** in **Chapter 4** is a diagram describing the complete model of the EAI's brain. **Figure 1** and **Figure 2** of **Chapter 2** explain the model, in stages.

Many senses capture information simultaneously, which initiate information streams. Each stream goes through its own series of deductions. Since there are many simultaneous streams of information, there are many series of deductions.

Table 2: The seven senses

The seven senses (inputs): seeing, hearing, touching, smelling, tasting, remembering and deducting.

The seven senses provide inputs (information) into deductions. The first five are well known. The additional two, although internal, provide just as much input as the other five senses. Remembering is previously recorded information that is retrieved, re-recorded and re-inputted in a deduction. Deducting is the ability to take information (from many senses) and link them, creating new/additional information to be recorded and re-inputted in a deduction. These are inputs of renewed or new information, like for the other five senses. Therefore, these are the sixth and seventh senses.

Table 3: The seven fundamental needs in order of priority

---

1 - Recording: The constant need to be alert for everything that indicates movement (noises, smells and vibrations) and to record what the senses observe.

2 - Linking: The constant need to create simple links with the content of the memory (deduction) including to link them to an emotion.

3 - Reacting: The constant need to react to emotions.

4 - Expulsing: The need to expulse undesirable internal elements (sweating, sneezing, coughing, spitting, excreting, etc.)

5 - Eating (energizing): The regular need for food (energy).

6 - Sleeping (repairing): The need to repair the body and clean/re-organize memory while sleeping (or inactive).

7 - Reproducing: The need for a reproductive partner or to create an offspring.

As in humans, the seven fundamental needs help prioritize the tasks in the EAI's brain. The fundamental needs also ensure that the EAI is functioning at all times, especially because the first three needs are constantly working. The first need is to record everything that moves or indicates movement (sound, smell or shaking), and this is the priority. Then it records items of focus depending on its needs and interests. All the senses are constantly on the lookout. Many senses capture information simultaneously, initiating many information streams. As we will see, the second need creates information in a useful manner such as *Valued information* (identifying the good), *Traumatisms* (identifying the bad), *Lived experiences*, *Knowledge*, *Groupings* and *Automatisms*. The third need finds reaction to an emotion and creates *Interests*. The second and third needs are implemented using deductions.

The fundamental needs are pre-programmed (i.e., innate) to indicate the priorities, but it allows the EAI to decide « Where, » « When » and « How » to satisfy its needs, as is the case for humans. In essence, this allows the EAI to have freewill.

Table 4: The seven fundamental emotions.

The seven emotions (reactions): interest (learning and acting), **pleasure** (continuing), **surprise** (seeking answer), **anger** (stopping and refusing), **fear** (protecting), **distress** (not knowing what to do) and **guilt** (not repeating past errors).

All the expressions used to express emotions found in dictionaries fall into seven groups, corresponding to the seven fundamental emotions. There are about 900 of these emotional adjectives and expressions (**Annex 1** and Annex 2). There are about 600 common names corresponding to these adjectives, and 500 verbs, as well as adverbs. About 60 % of the emotional expressions are not ambiguous, in that they clearly identify one of the seven fundamental emotions, at a given intensity. About 40 % of the expressions are ambiguous, meaning it requires context or asking the person if the word expresses for example, anger or guilt. Each of the 900 expressions are associated to one or many of the seven fundamental emotions with an intensity level of 1 to 10. The following **Table** gives some examples. The seven fundamental emotions are used in view of being more precise in identifying the need: (1) to search, (2) to refuse, (3) to protect, (4) to get help, (5) to not do it again, (6) to continue, or (7) to learn, discover, resolve, create, play or find entertainment.

Table 5: Emotional intensity expressed using adjectives – I am …
(The parentheses give the emotional intensity.)

- **Surprise**: Surprised (1), doubtful (3), undecided (4), confused (5), stunned (6), perplexed (7) amazed (8) dazed (9) and paralyzed (10).

- **Anger**: Not liking something (1), overworked (2), importuned (3), exasperated (4), treated unfairly (5), angry (6), irritated (7), revengeful (8), aggressive (9) and violent (10).

- **Fear**: Hesitating (1), suspicious (2), concerned (3), worried (4), fearful (5), intimidated (6), scared (7), frightened (8), brutalized (9), and panicked (10).

- **Distress**: Nonchalant (1), disorganized (2), without spirit (3), away (4), distressed (5), demoralized (6), sad (7), depressed (8), in tears (9) and suicidal (10).

- **Guilt**: Not proud (1), submitted (2), reproached (5), feeling liar (6), intrusive (7), shy (8), guilty (9) and shameful (10).

- **Pleasure**: Comfortable (1), satisfied (2), cheerful (3), self-assured (4), proud (5), happy (6), having fun (7), sensual (8), full of happiness (9) and overexcited (10).

- **Interest**: In acceptance (2), kind (3), interested (4), constructive (5), motivated (6), creative (7), curious (8), in need (9) and maniac (10).

There are seven types of information stored in the memory. Deductions create *Lived experience*, *Valued information*, *Knowledge*, *Traumatisms*, *Groupings* (categorization and generalisation of the information), *Automatisms* and *Interests* that activates the body.

Table 6: The seven types of information in the brain's memory

---

1 - Lived experiences: information captured from senses, and the chronology of our experiences.

2 - Valued information: information valued, as well as our personal values, beliefs, principles, prejudices, preferences and interests.

3 - Traumatisms: our experienced traumatisms, dangers, griefs, misfortunes, misery, troubles and guilts.

4 - Knowledge: Valued information that are linked, as well as our personal knowledge, lived experiences and abilities.

5 - Automatisms: our automatic reactions, those learned as well as those innate (pre-programmed).

6 - Groupings: our synonyms, translations, acronyms, abbreviations, categorisations, generalisations, etc.

7 - Interests: planned and prioritized needs, desires and interests to action and activate body parts.

Lived experiences: All information captured by the senses is chronologically recorded as a *Lived experience* and linked to an emotion and its intensity. The recording of information captured from the senses always includes the emotion and the intensity of this emotion. For each record, a deduction finds in EAI's memory the emotion to be linked to the record and its intensity. The emotion and its intensity allows for the classification and management of information according to their importance, and to recover them quickly based on their priority or importance.

If the same information is captured repeatedly, or repeats at other times, a deduction increases the intensity of the emotion for that record.

Valued information: Most of the information recorded in the *Lived experiences* is satisfactory, and the format of this recording is

IF an information **THEN PLEASURE** X

Here, X is the intensity of pleasure or satisfaction of the information varying say from 1 to 10. The information referred to here is the kind captured by one of the seven senses (e.g., seeing something, hearing something, etc.).

For example,

IF seeing the image of Mom's face **THEN PLEASURE** 10,

or

IF hearing a good song **THEN PLEASURE** 10.

The label **PLEASURE** here is a feeling of satisfaction. When the satisfaction reaches level 10, the EAI highly values the information. The simple repetition of an information increases this level up to 10. Therefore, for ease of retrieval, *Lived experiences* that have a high pleasure rating are known as *Valued information*. If this information were to trigger a *Traumatism*, trouble or even a surprise, a deduction would attach the troubling emotion instead of **PLEASURE**. A **PLEASURE** of intensity 10 maybe a belief, a principle of life, a personal value or simply a very useful knowledge. In other words, if an image, a sound, a speech, a touch, repeats itself, it is probably important to remember and probably useful. A deduction, however, can record erroneous information without the EAI's knowledge, as is the case for humans. Living experiences will fix these errors over time.

Traumatisms: When the stream from a sense records a troubling or traumatic information instead of a satisfactory or pleasing information, the emotion and its intensity are also recorded in a format similar to pleasure like this:

IF a satisfactory or pleasing information **THEN PLEASURE** X,

IF a troubling or traumatic information **THEN** (W, X),

where W is either the emotional label **SURPRISE, ANGER, FEAR, DISTRESS** or **GUILT**. X is still the intensity of the emotion varying from 1 to 10, and this intensity increases at each repetition. If the EAI is sensing pain, recording it, linking an emotion and an intensity to it, searching a solution to stop the pain and moving the body to solve the *Traumatism*; all in one thousandth of a second, then, every thousandth of a second the intensity of the *Traumatism* increases of 1 unity, and passes successively from surprise (seeking answer) 1 to 2, to 3, …, to 10, followed by anger (stopping and refusing) from 1 to 10, then to fear (protecting) from 1 to 10 and finally to distress (not knowing what to do) from 1 to 10. (In practice, the scale of the intensity could be 1 to 100, or 1 to 1000). A *Lived experience* tied to a traumatic emotion is called a *Traumatism*.

The Traumatism System: Each time there is a *Traumatism*, every thousandth of a second, the *Traumatism* evolves from **SURPRISE** 1 to 2, …, to 10, to **ANGER** from 1 to 10, then to **FEAR** from 1 to 10 and finally to **DISTRESS** from 1 to 10. This is the *Traumatism System*. Every thousandth of a second, a deduction searches a solution among the content of its memory (*Automatisms, Knowledge, Valued information, Groupings, other Traumatisms, Lived experiences,* and *Interests*). When it finds a solution, the current emotion and its intensity are recorded in the memory. If no solution is found, **DISTRESS** at level 10 is recorded, and the corresponding *Automatism* makes the body react (for example, an alarm or tears).

Table 7: *The Traumatism System.*

For a continuous pain or trouble, the emotion passes from **SURPRISE**, to **ANGER**, to **FEAR** and finally to **DISTRESS**, say, every thousandth of a second:

1- **IF** pain or trouble **THEN SURPRISE** X (a reaction to search in the memory)
2- **IF** pain or trouble **THEN ANGER** X (a reaction to refuse)
3- **IF** pain or trouble **THEN FEAR** X (a reaction to protect)
4- **IF** pain or trouble **THEN DISTRESS** X (a reaction to indicate a need of help)

where the intensity X increases, let say, from 1 to 1000 every thousandth of a second.

For example, suppose the EAI breaks one of its arms. When it realizes it cannot use its arm (using one of its senses or sensors), it is **SURPRISE** (in the first thousandths of a second). It seeks a solution in its memory, which depends on its *Automatisms* and *Knowledge* (e.g. to buy new parts to replace those broken), otherwise it is **ANGER**. In response to **ANGER**, it moves to find the solution, or ask for help. If it does not find a solution, it changes to **FEAR**. Now it shouts to receive or to find help, a solution or reinsurance. If it still has not resolved the *Traumatism*, it is in **DISTRESS** and an unintentional signal is sent automatically.

Guilt is a learned reaction, not an innate or pre-programmed reaction. The EAI learns not to hit when it has experienced to be hit and did not appreciate (as when learning not to bite when, after having bitten somebody, that person or somebody else bites us in return).

Knowledge: If two *Valued information* get recorded at the same time, a *Knowledge* is recorded in the memory, in the following format:

> **IF** an image **EQUALS** some sounds **THEN PLEASURE** X.

Here, X is the intensity of the pleasure of the equality and varies from 1 to 10. X increases by 1 each time both *Valued information* get recorded again at the same time.

As soon as the EAI is in function, a deduction records a link between an image and few sounds occurring simultaneously, as well as the emotion and its intensity. If the emotion is not traumatic, it saves satisfaction (i.e., **PLEASURE 1**). If the situation on the image and the simultaneous sounds is repeated, the intensity of the emotion is increased. For example, here is a solid *Knowledge* in the EAI's brain:

> **IF** an image of Mom **EQUALS** the sound « ma-ma » **THEN PLEASURE** 10.

If the EAI sees its mom (or its mentor), a deduction finds in its memory that it is linked to the sound « ma-ma », and the EAI hears the sound « ma-ma » in its head. If the EAI hears « ma-ma », another deduction finds the linked image and the EAI sees a picture of its mom in its head. That is, « ma-ma » is the definition of the image, and inversely the image is the definition of the word. The links (image-sounds) between images and sounds are *Knowledge* and these pairs constitute a large quantity of definitions of words and information.

If the coincidence of the two information is not repeated, the *Knowledge* will remain linked to a level of **PLEASURE** 1 and will not be used because it will be less important than other *Knowledge* linked to level 10. Only *Knowledge* linked to high satisfaction are used, as they take precedence.

Common nouns, proper nouns and adverbs: Not only common nouns and proper nouns are linked to images, but adjectives, verbs and adverbs as well. Many adverbs such as in front of, behind, right, left, up, down, over, under, away, close, etc., are linked to images in the following format:

> **IF** (an image of two objects in 3-D) **EQUALS** (an adverb) **THEN PLEASURE** X.

Verbs: Many verbs such as walking, climbing, descending, running, jogging, jumping, bumping, hitting, sliding, rolling, etc., are related to some images as follows:

> **IF** few images (or a video) of a moving object in relation to another object **EQUALS** (a verb) **THEN PLEASURE** X.

Adjectives: Many adjectives such as colours (blue, white, red, transparent, dark, pale, pastel, etc.), sizes (small, medium, large, tiny, huge, etc.), shapes (round, square, triangular, sharp, thin, fat, etc.), textures (soft, hard, rough, sticky, slippery, etc.), temperatures (warm, cold, hot, burning, etc.), weight (heavy, light, etc.) are linked to one or two images like this:

> **IF** one or two images **EQUALS** (an adjective) **THEN**

PLEASURE X.

All these images can be simple and small, without details, as in kid's cartoons.

Groupings: Regrouping information allows the EAI to efficiently store repetitive or similar information. The *Grouping System* achieves this by (G1) combining several information into a single concept, (G2) eliminating similar images in order to preserve only one (the last improved image being usually the best one), (G3) regrouping information that are synonymous, and (G4) regrouping information that is personally useful when linked.

The images captured by the vision that are similar or equal to a previously recorded image are filtered without saving duplication. They are improved by repetition (or concentration, which is equivalent) and the intensity of the satisfaction or *Traumatism* is increased. *Grouping* can involve the simplification of images, the generalization of images, filtration, or categorization. If in a similar image, a difference adds important information in view of the EAI's personal values, the difference is recorded. The words that have the same meaning (synonyms, translations, abbreviations, codes, etc.) are also grouped. The format of a *Grouping* is the following:

> **IF** « word 1» or image 1 **EQUALS** (« word 2 », « word 3 », image 2, image of a word) **THEN PLEASURE** X.

Stereotype and prejudice: When a word is linked to a generalized image, it is a stereotype. This can create a bias, or prejudice.

Automatisms: As the word implies, an *Automatism* is a series of automated actions. A minimum of *Automatisms* are pre-programmed (i.e., innate). As soon as the EAI is on, it reacts to fundamental needs and emotions, by automatically activating an appropriate *Automatism* to address the fundamental need or emotion. Initial *Automatisms* are simple but will evolve over time. For example, the initial *Automatism* for **PLEASURE** simply means to continue what it does. For **ANGER** (to refuse) is to move the limbs, **FEAR** (to protect itself) is to shout, **DISTRESS** (not knowing what to do) is to produce a visible signal (like tears are for humans). The EAI will always be curious and interested (*Interest* is the default emotion because deductions will constantly create links). It has the interest to play, learn and resolve the *Traumatisms*. The *Automatism* to the EAI's emotions will evolve according to its *Lived experiences* and *Knowledge*.

Automatisms are learned by trial and error, and also by imitating others, sometimes unconsciously, for example, by recording what others are doing and saying. By the mere repetition of seeing the behaviour of others, this behaviour is recorded and learned as a *Valued information* and thereby replicated by the brain. An *Automatism* often becomes a personal value (**PLEASURE** of intensity 10). An *Automatism* is a behaviour or skill that is created by the repetition of body movements. The EAI learns them using deductions that create *Valued information*, *Knowledge*, *Groupings*, as well as *Traumatisms* to correct and improve the *Automatism*. These *Automatisms* are as much those of habits, sportsmen, workers, professionals, careers, social behaviour, language, communication, etc. Many streams and deductions create links of the following types, using trial and error, to create an *Automatism*:

> **IF** an image of the teacher's arm **THEN PLEASURE** 10,

> **IF** the image of EAI's arm **EQUALS ALMOST** (i.e. similar to) the image of teacher's arm **THEN PLEASURE** X,

> **IF** the image of EAI's arm **IS NOT EQUAL TO** (i.e. is not similar to) the image of teacher's arm **THEN ANGER** 1, and

> **IF ANGER** 1 **THEN** move (randomly using trials and errors), and

> **IF** the image of EAI's arm **EQUALS** (i.e., simultaneously) (**IF** feeling the contraction of the shoulder muscle **THEN PLEASURE** X, **IF** feeling the contraction of the elbow muscle **THEN ANGER** 1, **IF** feeling the contraction of the wrist muscle **THEN PLEASURE** X) **THEN PLEASURE** 1.

At the end, an *Automatism* takes the following format:

> **IF** an image of EAI's arm **EQUALS** (feeling the contraction of the shoulder muscle, feeling the contraction of the elbow muscle, feeling the contraction of the wrist muscle) **THEN PLEASURE** 10.

Throughout its life, an *Automatism* can be improved, and a copy may be modified to perform another task, such as to take a glass, take a pencil, drive a car, throw a ball, etc.

Eventually, the EAI mimics speaking aloud using an *Automatism*, and says out loud "ma-ma". The link in its memory encouraging this faculty is this:

> **IF** the teacher says « bra-vo » and the teacher smiles **THEN PLEASURE** 10.

> **IF** the EAI says « ma-ma » (even by accident) **EQUALS** (the teacher says « bra-vo » and the teacher smiles) **THEN PLEASURE** X.

Initially, an *Automatism* creates simple sentences: « verb », or « subject-verb », or « subject-verb-complement ». A simple Automatism builds questions, by adding « Who », « What », « Where », « When », « How », « Why » and « How » in front of « is it that » followed by a sentence « subject-verb » or « subject-verb-complement ».

The EAI develops *Automatisms* to build more complex sentences, for example, sentences containing « several subjects - several verbs - several complements », and this, by listening to others, and reading. It learns to reverse the order in sentences, to play with words, replacing parts with synonyms and metaphors, using imaged description, stories, adding drama into sentences, etc. Finally, it creates and manipulates abstract concepts.

If the EAI hears « 1 + 1 = 3. » It searches in its memory, finds **IF** « 1 + 1 = 2 » **THEN PLEASURE 10**. It will thus record **IF** « 1 + 1 = 3 » **THEN ANGER 1**, and in reaction to its anger a deduction finds an *Automatism* to say « No, » or « It's wrong, » or « It's 2, » or « 1 + 1 = 2, » upon its *Lived experiences* and situation.

Interests: The *Interests* are the information that activates EAI's body parts. It's a list of things to do. It's the list of long-term interests, medium term, short term, those for today, for the next hour, and also those for the coming milliseconds. The list is dynamic, constantly re-prioritized, some *Interests* are waiting to be activated, others activate various body parts.

The *Automatisms* that will activate the body are copied as needed on the *Interests*. They come from deductions. Many *Automatisms* may be copied simultaneously. Hence, there is a pile of *Automatisms* within the *Interests* requesting to activate the body. There is also the innate *Automatisms* of the fundamental needs that are permanently stored in the *Interests* and always active. The first line of one of the *Automatisms* located in the *Interests* activates the body (for example, to move the shoulder). If there is satisfaction (success), the first line is deleted from the stack (not from the memory), the 2nd line is activated (move the elbow) and then the 3rd line (move the wrist) etc. There are several *Automatisms* activated at the same time (for example, for the vision, hearing, touch, to adjust the walking and balance, for the movement of the arms, head, to speak, to create sentences, to think, to understand, etc., all at the same time). There is a stream for each of these actions. There is an *Automatism* in each information stream. A stream, for one information, (for example, to adjust the ankle during walking) goes through the *Interests*, which initiates the movement of a body part. According to this movement, the senses capture information, which is recorded. This can initiate several new streams, or no new stream. A deduction within the stream checks the resulting requested movement and links an emotion to it. A second deduction decides, depending on the emotion, if one or many *Automatisms* are copied onto the *Interests*. This can initiate several new streams or not. (See **Chapter 2** and **Annex 3** for a detailed explanation of the *Interests*).

Deductions: With many senses providing inputs simultaneously, which all need to be recorded, analyzed and processed; *deductions* handles these tasks. There is not one deduction system, but a series of three types of deduction in each cycle of each stream. There is the *Deduction type no 1a*, the *Deduction type no 1b* and the *Deduction type no 2* (see **DT1a, DT1b** and **DT2** in **Figure 2** and **Figure** 3). A **DT1a** creates a *Valued information* or a *Traumatism*. A **DT1b** creates a *Knowledge, Grouping* or *Automatism*. A **DT2** identifies the reaction to an emotion and creates an *Interest*. The senses create simultaneously many streams of information. For example, many streams are necessary to analyze images and videos, to produce and process conversations, as well as to create ideas. There are thus many simultaneous deductions occurring every millisecond.

Each stream consists of several cycles. Each cycle goes through the *Interests*, followed by moving a body part, then capturing an information using one of the senses, recording the information into the *Lived experiences*, regrouping the information (creating *Groupings*), and then going through a series of deductions. **DT1b** links two information from two streams to create or retrieve and improve a *Knowledge, Grouping or Automatism*. **DT1a** identifies the traumatic emotion located in the memory connected to this information, and links this emotion (if not, the emotion **PLEASURE**) to the information creating a *Traumatism* (if not, a *Valued information*). **DT2** finds in the memory the response to this emotion by selecting and copying an *Automatism* back onto the *Interests*. Streams and cycles are shown in **Figure 1** and **Figure** 2 (**Chapter 2**) and in **Figure 3** (**Chapter 4**).

In view of building an EAI, the only components to be programmed, apart from the usual management of cameras, earphones, speakers, databases, energy and maintenance requirements, are the 1st fundamental need (recordings), the *Groupings* system, the 2nd fundamental need (**DT1a** and **DT1b**) and the 3rd fundamental need (**DT2**). Here are the programming needs:

The memory contains at the beginning the *Automatisms* contained in **Table 11** plus those in **Chapter 6**. These *Automatisms* ensure the functioning of the EAI. The unfulfillment of any of the first three fundamental needs will demand a movement of the body.

DT1a takes the just recorded *Lived experience* and tries to find if it corresponds to an activated line within the *Interests,* thereby confirming that the action was taken. If it succeeds, it is satisfactory, it erases (or deactivates) that line and activates the subsequent line. Otherwise, it finds the information in the memory that is equal, similar or synonymous (using the *Grouping System*) and recovers it. Tied to it, is the emotional label to feel. It records this label (to the *Lived experience*, making the *Lived experience* a *Valued information* or a *Traumatism*) and increases its intensity. It records the label "**ANGER**" if the *Lived experience* is the negation of an existing *Valued information*.

The *Grouping System* creates G1, G2, G3, and G4 *Groupings* as explained above.

DT1b links two pieces of information recorded simultaneously. It records the emotional label "**PLEASURE**", creating a *Knowledge*, or increases the emotional intensity. When the image of a recorded *Knowledge* is accessed, it pronounces in the internal speaker the words linked to it. When the words of a recorded *Knowledge* are accessed, it displays on the internal display the image linked to it. Finally, it ties the label "**ANGER**" to the *Lived experience* if it is the negation of one of the two *Valued information* defining a *Knowledge*.

DT2 chooses the *Automatism* to respond to the emotion, based on the emotion, intensity, situation and memory content, and sends a copy to the *Interests*.

The details are explained in the book.

Chapter 2: How the EAI brain functions

In this chapter, a first overview of the EAI's brain function is presented using **Figure 1** and **Figure** 2 exposing in detail half of the EAI's 29 components. This chapter also shows the first information contained in the EAI's memory at the beginning of its existence, the format of the information to be recorded in the EAI's memory, and how the EAI will auto-program itself in view of managing its sensors as well as its motors that will make it move, talk and think.

If nature created a form of intelligence in animals, it is primarily to ensure the animal's survival. Based on this fact, each of the 29 components mentioned above in **Table 1** will be defined in order to ensure the EAI's survival. In addition, each of the 29 components will have a different utility than the others and each will be required to allow its survival. Each component will thus have its importance in the functioning of the EAI's intelligence, brain and body.

Figure 1 shows the relationship between the memory content, the five usual senses and the movement of the body parts. This is what the arrows 1, 2 and 3 indicate, and this, in the clockwise direction. (1) The memory content influences the movement of several body parts. (2) The movement of the body influences what many of the senses will capture, and (3), the senses capture many information, which influences the content of the memory. To pass through steps 1, 2 and 3 constitutes one cycle in the brain streams.

Figure 1: The brain's cycle and streams

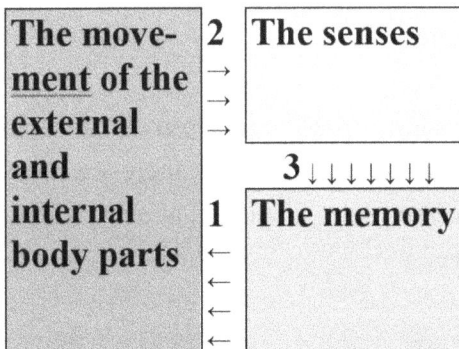

Figure 1 displays several arrows at each step for the following reasons: At step (1), the memory content decides to move several parts of the body simultaneously. At step (2), several senses operate simultaneously and can capture much information at the same time. In step (3), various information is recorded simultaneously in the memory. If while I walk on the sidewalk, I listen to a conversation and I feel a hollow in my stomach because I am hungry, I turn my head and smell a pizzeria, but I knock someone and apologize, there are several parts of my body that are moving simultaneously. The movement of my body causes many senses to work at the same time. Not only do sight, hearing, smell and touch function simultaneously, but also there are several pieces of information coming from a single sense simultaneously. For example, information from the touch of the right leg, left leg, right arm, left arm, knee, ankle, hand, neck, stomach and bumping against someone are all recorded independently and simultaneously through the sense of touch in step (3) to then be processed in memory.

A single arrow in step (3) corresponds to a small bit of information that comes from one sense in step (2). For example, the sense of touch that captures the pressure on the right ankle, say, for a millisecond. This little information is stored in memory and processed. If this information requires adjustment of the body movement, this decision is sent to step (1) the movement of the body. Walking on the sidewalk, steps (1), (2) and (3) are repeated at a high speed (say every thousandth of a second), and this series of cycles on the right ankle is a stream of information. There are several information streams operating simultaneously, several for conversation (and hearing), others for the vision and the sense of touch (internal and external). This is what the arrows in **Figure 1** display. Each stream (one or more for each sense) may contain one or more cycles. A cycle may end at steps (1) (2) or (3) for all sorts of reasons.

We can also track the stream of information in **Figure 2** (also clockwise). To avoid cluttering the **Figure**, and to remember that there are many streams running simultaneously, two arrows are displayed at every step.

Figure 2: The initial functioning of the brain

(Follow the series of two arrows in the clockwise direction. The two arrows indicate that there are several streams running simultaneously. Steps 1, 2 and 3 show a complete cycle.)

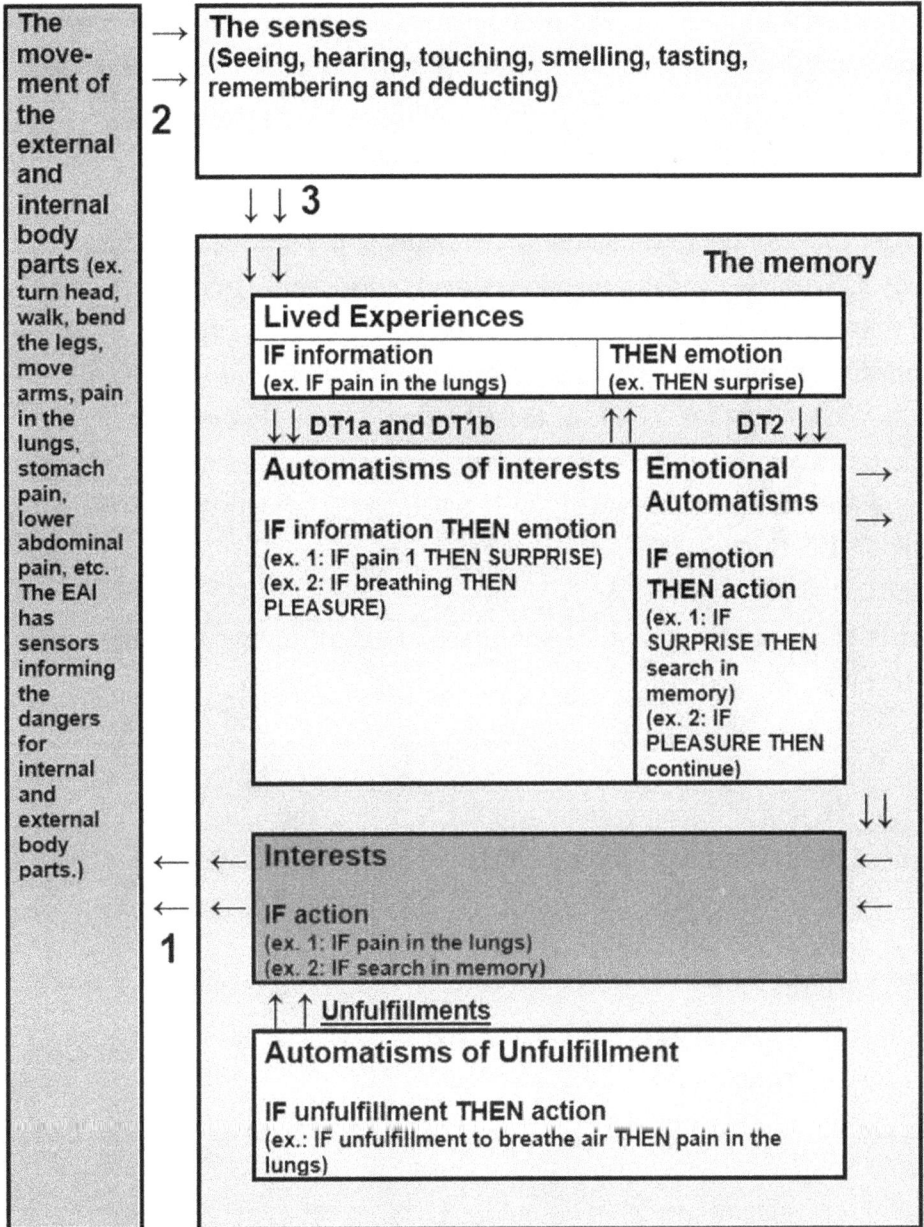

The move-ment of the external and internal body parts (ex. turn head, walk, bend the legs, move arms, pain in the lungs, stomach pain, lower abdominal pain, etc. The EAI has sensors informing the dangers for internal and external body parts.)

→ → **2**

The senses
(Seeing, hearing, touching, smelling, tasting, remembering and deducting)

↓ ↓ **3**

↓ ↓   **The memory**

Lived Experiences

IF information	THEN emotion
(ex. IF pain in the lungs)	(ex. THEN surprise)

↓↓ **DT1a and DT1b**   ↑↑   **DT2** ↓↓

Automatisms of interests	**Emotional Automatisms**
IF information THEN emotion (ex. 1: IF pain 1 THEN SURPRISE) (ex. 2: IF breathing THEN PLEASURE)	IF emotion THEN action (ex. 1: IF SURPRISE THEN search in memory) (ex. 2: IF PLEASURE THEN continue)

→ →

↓↓

Interests

1

IF action
(ex. 1: IF pain in the lungs)
(ex. 2: IF search in memory)

← ← ← ←

↑ ↑ **Unfulfillments**

Automatisms of Unfulfillment

IF unfulfillment THEN action
(ex.: IF unfulfillment to breathe air THEN pain in the lungs)

33

Although the goal is to create an EAI, it is difficult to explain the EAI's design without using human fundamental needs and behaviours. In other words, by removing from the model the needs to sleep (getting repaired), eat, eliminate undesirable internal elements (sweating, sneezing, coughing, spitting, excreting, etc.) and to reproduce, we will wonder why other components work as proposed here. Human needs, which nevertheless add complexity to the brain function, facilitate and simplify the understanding of the model. Once the model is understood, it is possible to omit certain fundamental needs and perhaps senses (e.g., tasting and smelling) in order to implement an EAI. However, it is by creating a design containing 29 components that the EAI is completely modelled.

So, let us begin the explanation of the model at the time of birth, where the body arrives already fully functional, ready to survive. Humans already have an *Automatism* for **breathing**, **digesting**, and another to **expulse undesirable internal elements**. These are primary fundamental needs. If there is a failure to meet one of these three needs, an *Automatism* causes pain or discomfort to the lungs, abdomen, or lower abdomen. These needs and *Automatisms* are shown in **Table 8** using simple algorithm links « **IF this THEN that** ».

Table 8: Six innate *Automatisms*: three of unfulfillment and three of interest

---

IF unfulfillment to breathe **THEN** pain in the lungs
IF unfulfillment to digest **THEN** pain in the abdomen
IF unfulfillment to expulse **THEN** pain in the lower abdomen

IF breathing **THEN PLEASURE**
IF digesting **THEN PLEASURE**
IF expulse **THEN PLEASURE**

Again, I recognize that humans and EAI's basic needs may be different because of their physiology. However, the logic is the same. For example, the need for a source of energy is a fundamental need. For humans, it is food, for the EAI, it is a battery. Using these analogies to the basic needs of the human brain allows us to better understand the model and the system of intelligence, consciousness, motivation and freewill.

In the model, the majority of the information stored in the memory consists of two columns of information: (**IF** this, **THEN** that). The deductions will search through billions of such simple logical relations « **IF this THEN that**. » The information contained in the columns (1) comes from senses or sensors (for example, perceiving a lack of oxygen to breathe, stomach pain, seeing something, hearing sounds, feeling pleasure, etc.), or (2) is a reaction that can be produced using a motor (e.g., breathing, stomach pain, moving a muscle or limb, pleasure, etc.). A motor produces breathing. If a sensor perceives the breath, the engine is encouraged to continue breathing. In other words, a motor that produces pleasure simply continues the action, since it did not meet troubles or *Traumatisms* (not encountering troubles is sensing pleasure or satisfaction).

Humans also need to eat to have energy and to grow. Another need is to sleep in view of cleaning the memory, eliminating toxins, repairing and building cells in the body and thus growing. For these two needs (eating and sleeping), humans' *Automatisms* cause to feel, through the sense of internal touch, a hollow in the stomach and feeling slow, while in the other case, yawning and having heavy eyelids. Again, the memory contains the corresponding *Automatisms* represented by the links in **Table 9**.

Table 9: Four other innate *Automatisms*: two of unfulfillment and two of interest

---

IF unfulfillment to eat **THEN** discomfort in the stomach
IF unfulfillment to sleep **THEN** heavy eyelids

IF eating **THEN PLEASURE** (to energize)
IF sleeping **THEN PLEASURE** (to repair)

We have just seen that the information pre-stored in the memory about unfulfilling the basic needs will have the following form: **IF** there is an unfulfillment of a basic need **THEN** there is an action; or simply

IF an unfulfillment THEN action.   (Equation 1)

Furthermore, the information links regarding the basic needs themselves will have, as seen above, the following form:

IF a basic need THEN PLEASURE.   (Equation 2)

The unfulfillment links to basic needs (Equation 1) and the basic need links (Equation 2) are *Automatisms* that will dictate the action of the body at the right time. Each of these links is also a simple information stored in memory (sometimes involving programming lines). We see these *Automatisms* in **Figure 2**. For example, when there is an unfulfillment, the action related to it is copied to a region in the memory I call the *Interests*. One of the arrows next to the word "**Unfulfillments**" in **Figure 2** indicates that the action of an *Automatism* is copied to the *Interests*. This action of an *Automatism* may contain multiple actions (therefore several programming lines), such as yawning and blinking eyelids. Once the instructions are in the *Interests* the first programming line initiates a stream and sends a signal to an external or internal part of the body, to yawn, and the second line introduces another stream to blink eyelids, etc.

From the streams coming out from the *Interests*, body parts get activated (step 1 in **Figure 2**). There are movements of the body (e.g., eyelids blinking, head turns, walking, etc.) and movements within the body that cannot be seen but is felt by the sense of internal touch (for example, pain in the lungs). Naturally, the movement of the external and internal parts of the body influences what can be observed using the senses (step 2 in **Figure 2**). The senses observe the external and internal environment of the body and record it in memory (step 3 in **Figure 2**).

The fundamental needs of the brain are *Automatisms* stored in the memory at birth that initiate streams and trigger actions on the body (step 1).

If at the time of birth, a baby cannot breathe because of the mucus in the mouth, then they experience pain in the lungs. This is a first unfulfillment of a fundamental need (see the bottom box in **Figure 2**). This unfulfillment is copied onto the *Interests* and it activates the body (step 1 in **Figure 2**). The sense of touch captures internal pain (step 2). The memory is made aware of the pain (step 3). Since the baby has never felt this pain, its memory does not contain any information about this pain, thus its memory does not contain « **IF pain in the lungs**. »

What is then its reaction? (1) The first sensation of pain is related to a reaction *to search his memory*. (2) If the same pain persists, it is related to a reaction *to refuse*. Then (3), if the pain becomes more intense in the same place it is the reaction *to protect themselves* which takes over, until (4) the reaction *to indicate distress* if nothing is done to help them. These four reactions come from *Automatisms* also recorded in the memory at birth. These are emotional reactions respectively named *surprise, anger, fear* and *sadness*. The ascending order of these possible *Traumatisms* in a newborn is given in **Table 10**. These expressions of emotions commonly used are connected to reactions and *Automatisms* very clearly defined in **Chapter 8**.

Table 10 : Ascending order of *Traumatism* – *The Traumatism System*

IF pain 1 **THEN SURPRISE** (a reaction to search in the memory)
IF pain 2 **THEN ANGER** (a reaction to refuse)
IF pain 3 **THEN FEAR** (a reaction to protect itself)
IF pain 4 **THEN DISTRESS** (a reaction to indicate the need of help).

Every emotion is accompanied by the energy to deal with the situation. This dose of energy is greater or less depending on the intensity of the *Traumatism*. A repetition of the *Traumatism* amplifies the intensity. If pain recurs, the intensity of the emotion is increased in a scale of, say, 1 to 10, as follows:

IF pain 2 **THEN ANGER** 1

IF pain 2 **THEN ANGER** 2

IF pain 2 **THEN ANGER** 3

IF pain 2 **THEN ANGER** 4

IF pain 2 **THEN ANGER** 5

IF pain 2 **THEN ANGER** 6

IF pain 2 **THEN ANGER** 7

IF pain 2 **THEN ANGER** 8

IF pain 2 **THEN ANGER** 9

IF pain 2 **THEN ANGER** 10

A level 1 represents a low intensity of emotion, while levels 2, 3, 4, etc., are higher intensities. Thus, at each cycle of a stream, thus every thousandth of a second, the intensity of an emotion increases by 1 unit. When the *surprise* reaches level 10, the emotion passes to *anger* (1 to 10), followed by *fear* (1 to 10) to finish with *distress* (1 to 10). Perhaps in practice, the range will be from 1 to 100 or 1000.

Physical reactions related to emotions are common to all babies and are physiological reactions (hence, motors): a baby has the *Automatism* to move its limbs and head. This behaviour is sometimes due to denial, *anger*. The baby possesses the *Automatism* to scream, this reaction is associated with *fear*. When they let tears flow, it is related to *sadness (distress)*. When they are searching in their memory, staying still, it is the *surprise*. Depending on the intensity of the pain, the movement, screams, crying and searching in its memory will be more virulent. Initially, it is sufficient that the memory of the baby contains 19 pre-programmed *Automatisms* to indicate its fundamental needs as well as its reactions to emotions as shown in **Table 11**. The EAI's memory will possess at the beginning some of this information. These are automatic reactions that are not learned but innate, thus pre-programmed.

Like the basic needs, reactions to the emotions are, at the beginning of the existence, innate and pre-programmed *Automatisms* stored in memory, which activates the body (step 1). However, unlike the basic needs that are immutable, *Automatisms* related to emotions will change over time in accordance with the recorded *Lived experiences*.

Table 11: Summary of *Automatisms* at birth: 5 of unfulfillment, 5 of needs, 4 of *Traumatism* and 5 of emotional reactions

(The information and actions in uppercase are immutable.)

IF unfulfillment THEN action:
IF unfulfillment to breathe **THEN** pain in the lungs
IF unfulfillment to digest **THEN** pain in the abdomen
IF unfulfillment to expulse **THEN** pain in the lower abdomen
IF unfulfillment to eat **THEN** discomfort in the stomach
IF unfulfillment to sleep **THEN** heavy eyelids

IF fundamental need THEN PLEASURE:
IF BREATHE **THEN PLEASURE**
IF EAT **THEN PLEASURE**
IF DIGEST **THEN PLEASURE**
IF EXPULSE **THEN PLEASURE**
IF SLEEP **THEN PLEASURE**

IF pain THEN Traumatism:
IF PAIN 1 **THEN** SURPRISE
IF PAIN 2 **THEN** ANGER
IF PAIN 3 **THEN** FEAR
IF PAIN 4 **THEN** DISTRESS (sadness)

IF Traumatism THEN action:
IF SURPRISE **THEN** search another link in memory
IF ANGER **THEN** move the head and limbs
IF FEAR **THEN** scream
IF DISTRESS **THEN** flow tears

IF PLEASURE THEN CONTINUE

To understand what happens in the memory during a cycle, the example of a baby needing air to breathe at birth is taken again here by following one by one the arrows in **Figure 2.** The *Automatism* of unfulfilling the need to breathe air **"THEN pain in the lungs"** is copied to the *Interests* in the format **"IF pain in the lungs"** (see **Figure 2**). An arrow ↑ to the left of the word **"Unfulfillments"** represents the action of copying. This new information found on the *Interests* initiates a movement in the lungs that creates pain (see step 1 in **Figure 2**). The information observed by the senses (here, the pain in the lungs signalled by the sense of internal touch, see step 2 in **Figure 2**) is registered as an information in a part of memory called the *Lived experiences* (see step 3 in **Figure 2**). The new information recorded in the *Lived experiences* of the memory is **"IF pain in the lungs"** (see **Figure 2**).

The deduction comes in. A first deduction searches in the memory the information **"IF pain in the lungs"**. The baby's memory contains at birth only the *Automatisms* found in **Table 11**. Since the baby has never had pain to the lungs, the deduction does not find **"IF pain in the lungs"** anywhere in the memory. What happens then when the baby lives pain? The deduction finds an information called **"a first pain"** that is **"IF PAIN 1 THEN SURPRISE 1"**. This link in the brain tells it that if it feels pain it should first be surprised. The body is not yet activated for the surprise. We are still in the memory. This deduction **"IF PAIN 1 THEN SURPRISE 1"** is represented by an arrow ↓ to the left of the *Deduction type no 1a* (**DT1a**) in **Figure 2**. This same *Automatism* records the emotion and intensity **"SURPRISE 1"** in the *Lived experiences*, next to the **"IF pain in the lungs"** information, indicated by an arrow ↑ to the right of **DT1a** in **Figure 2**. The part of memory called the *Lived experiences* now contains **"IF pain in the lungs THEN SURPRISE 1"**. This is the first information created in the memory thanks to a *Deduction type 1a*. This is how the brain starts recording new information, and how it will auto-program itself during its life.

Then comes a second deduction that tells it how to react to the surprise. The second deduction is represented by an arrow ↓ at the right of **DT2**. The second deduction searches in the entire contents of the memory what to do when "**surprised**." This deduction automatically searches the emotion "SURPRISE" in the "**IF**" of the memory. It finds "**IF SURPRISE THEN search another link in the memory**". This *Automatism* copies "**search another link in the memory**" on the *Interests* in the format "**IF search another link ...**". This expression now activates the body (step 1) in view of finding what to do with such a pain. The *Automatism* of surprise seeks another link. Once again, in this new cycle, it finds nothing (because it never felt this pain before), and the senses observe nothing but pain to the lungs. We have just explained a complete cycle of operation of the brain. Fortunately, another stream, the *Automatism* of the fundamental need to breathe, is still present on the *Interests*. The brain tries to breathe, it is still not breathing, it still feels pain (step 2 and 3).

We are in the second cycle (step 3), **DT1a** finds "**If PAIN 1 THEN SURPRISE 2**" (the intensity of surprise increased from 1 to 2). The cycles continue. At the eleventh cycle, **DT1a** finds "**IF PAIN 2 THEN ANGER 1**"; he feels the chemistry of anger. **DT2** finds the *Automatism* of anger "**IF ANGER THEN move the arms and head**", which is copied onto the *Interests* that activates the head and limbs (step 1), but he is still in pain (step 2 and 3).

We are in the 21st cycle (step 3). **DT1a** and **DT2** find "**IF PAIN 3 THEN FEAR 1**" and "**IF FEAR THEN scream**" respectively. He tries to scream, the mucus is cleared, he screams, and finally he breathes. Now the senses of touch and smell indicate that he is breathing (step 2). He records in his *Lived experiences* that he breathes (step 3) and he finds "**IF BREATHING THEN PLEASURE 1**". The *Automatism* of pleasure "**IF PLEASURE THEN continue**" tells him to continue the stack of *Interests*, thus to continue breathing (step 1) but also to clear from the stack, the interests to scream, move and search for another link (however, the original *Automatisms* still exist in memory). He is calming. The *Automatism* to breathe, found on the *Interests*, will not stop anymore, and other interests will get activated in parallel, onto other streams. Again, we have just gone through the complete loop of the brain's functionality, many times. This example and **Figure 2** explain the two steps of deduction (**DT1a** followed by **DT2**) and give an overview of the function of the brain. Nearly half of the 29 components were represented here.

At each observation recorded in the memory, there are two deductions. First, a deduction **DT1a** that binds the information observed to the relation "**IF the information was lived in the pass THEN the emotion lived in the pass and its intensity**" and this identifies the emotion to link to the information observed. Secondly, the deduction **DT2** that binds this emotion to the following relation "**IF an emotion THEN an action**." When this action is copied onto the *Interests*, the body is activated, which causes it to move, scream or shed tears.

While programming lines record what the senses capture, make deductions, and manage motors, sensors and information in memory; note that we will pre-program only the 29 components, all the other EAI's behaviours will auto-program themselves, as is the case for humans.

In summary, we remember that each cycle of **Figure 2** takes a fraction of a second, say one thousandth of a second. There are several senses that functions simultaneously. Each sense produces its own stream of cycles. One sense may occupy multiple streams. What must be remembered here is that there are a large number of cycles, and a large number of streams.

Here are the reasons and benefits for which nature has intended two steps of deduction. **DT1a** which registers an emotion to the event allows to make this information readily available for future events. At a future event, **DT1a** finds without delay whether to either search for another link, refuse, protect itself, to not do it again, to ask for help or to continue. However, it does not say how to do it. To decide how to do it, takes time; and depending on the intensity, it is possible that there is little time available to react. (Sometimes we say we have reacted too quickly, without thinking.) Second, **DT1a** also allows the stream to increase the intensity of emotion at each cycle when the problem persists. Third, the second step, **DT2**, provides the opportunity to change the action to be taken to respond to the emotion, and thus to decide, and this at every cycle. This double deduction system therefore provides a freedom of choice and an ability to better respond to our survival. (The ability to react instantly is always available.) Finally, this system allows to record the maximum intensity that the emotion reached when the emotion was resolved. Let us say the child finally recorded **"IF pain to the lungs THEN FEAR 4"** where 4 is the intensity of the fear. The next time the child has pain in the lung (e.g. when diving underwater), the deduction **DT1a** will find **"IF pain to the lungs THEN FEAR 4"**. He will begin his fear response to that intensity. This would explain why people react to a situation with an anger or fear of great intensity while for others the reaction is different. The content of the brain explains the behaviour of individuals.

In the next chapter, changing a behaviour following an emotional *Traumatism* or pleasure is explained through imitation and language. For now, **DT1a** and **DT2** are sufficient to meet the fundamental needs and their unfulfillment.

Finally, **Figure 2** provides an overview of a practical model of the brain in order to create an EAI. This figure explains and demonstrates the brain's functionality at birth. At this time, the memory contains the *Automatisms* of **Table 11**, which include the *Traumatisms* System (**Table 10**). Some components and *Automatisms* are still missing, but will be added in the next chapters.

Summary

Here is, in summary, what the cycle describing how the brain functions tells us. (1) The *unfulfillment of the fundamental needs* decides when to send some *Automatisms* to the body. (2) These *Automatisms* influence the *movement of the external and internal body parts*. (3) The movement of the body influences what the *senses* observe. (4) These *senses* observe the external and internal environment of the body. (5) These observations coming from the senses are stored in memory. (6) Each information recorded is linked to an *emotion* using a *first deduction*. This adds a new record in memory. (7) This *emotion* is related to an *Automatism*, using a *second deduction*. (8) This *Automatism* is copied to the *Interests* which activates the body. And we return to step (2). If the brain records an external event, this information is introduced into the cycle at step (4). This cycle is represented in **Figure 2**. There are several such cycles occurring simultaneously in the brain. If the same cycle continues repeating itself, it is a stream. The EAI will function according to this cycle.

This chapter introduced the format of the information contained in the EAI's brain. We find this format in **Table 11** . This table contains *emotions*, *Traumatisms* and *fundamental needs* (to be adapted to the EAI's physiology) that will be found in the EAI's memory at the start of its existence. The *Traumatism System* (**Table 10**) and how deductions occur (**DT1a** and **DT2**) were explained. About half of the deduction types, emotions, fundamental needs and 29 components modeling the EAI were introduced here.

Chapter 3: How the brain acquires Valued information, Knowledge, Groupings, Automatisms, imitation and Language

This chapter describes four key components that allow the EAI to create, manage and optimize its knowledge and skills. Those are:

1- The *Valued information*,
2- The *Knowledge*,
3- The *Groupings* and
4- The *Automatisms*.

Because the *Emotional Artificial Intelligence* (EAI) is modeled with very similar capabilities to humans, it learns through the same stages of life. It will learn by playing in the early years of its life. Then it will pass the exams of primary, secondary, college and university. Since it does not need to eat and sleep, it will learn 24 hours a day, 7 days a week, thus in much less time than a human will. After a few years, it will be a specialist. In addition, we must take into account that once an EAI has learnt a certain task, we can make copies of it.

It's impossible to pre-program all the skills, speeches, knowledge and reactions necessary to cope with the many situations that the EAI will face throughout its life. To build this EAI, only the 29 components have to be assembled or taken into account, and only the recordings, deductions and *Grouping System* will need to be pre-programmed. For the rest, the EAI will auto-program itself, as humans do.

Following the pre-programmed (innate) abilities of **Chapter 2**, the EAI continues to evolve and learn for itself by recording information, as we do. The EAI's memory is a digital database limited in space and in energy. The memory space, the recorded information and the speed of action and reaction must be optimized, as is the case for our brain. This chapter explains how nature has completed this feat.

We start by giving a summary of the four components explained in this chapter to provide a vision of what to expect in this chapter.

All information stored in memory, however small, are linked to an emotion. This ability is necessary to decide whether the EAI should keep or reject even the slightest information. This necessity becomes evident when reading the chapter. The simplest recorded information will always be a pair of (information, emotion). The information is connected either to a traumatic emotion and its intensity (see *Traumatisms* in **Chapter 2**), or to a pleasure (a satisfaction) and its intensity (see **Table 11** of **Chapter 2**). The majority of the information is pleasant or satisfactory. For example, the sound "ma-ma" and the image of Mom are linked to pleasure, therefore stored as *Valued information* represented in the following format:

A Valued Information:

      IF an information **THEN PLEASURE X.**   (Equation 3)

The variable X is a number between 1 and 10. It represents an intensity level of the satisfaction of the information. Data associated with intensity 1 will eventually be forgotten. Those linked to an intensity of 10 becomes an acquired information, a principle of life, a personal value, a belief, a stereotype, a prejudice, etc. By varying from 1 to 10, an information is more or less valued, thus the name, a *Valued information*.

The majority of records in the memory consist of *Valued information*. Links between *Valued information* are also recorded to create the three other components: The *Knowledge*, the *Groupings* and the *Automatisms*. These links of *Knowledge, Groupings* and *Automatisms* are also associated with an intensity of emotion 1 to 10, as in the following equations.

A *Knowledge* is created when two *Valued Information*, for example, the sound « ma-ma » and the image of Mom, are linked together. The link formed between the two is represented by the following equation:

A *Knowledge*:

> **IF** an information A **EQUALS** an information B **THEN**
> **PLEASURE X**   (Equation 4)

where information A is different from information B, and X is the degree of satisfaction of the equality.

For the EAI as for humans, it is essential to minimize the amount of stored information and optimize the compilation and use of such information, if only to decrease the amount of energy, memory space, processing of images and texts (speech) required for its functioning. The means to reduce energy consumption and optimize the EAI's functioning are drawn again from the example of the human brain. The means consist to group the information to meet four requirements, which are:

> 1- To group several information into a single concept,
> 2. To group and filter similar images to preserve only one,
> 3- To group information that are synonymous,
> 4- To group information having personally a useful link.

The format of a *Grouping* is the following:

A *Grouping*:

> **IF** information A **EQUALS** (information B,
> information C, information D, information E, etc.)
> **THEN PLEASURE X**   (Equation 5)

where the information A, B, C, etc., are all different, and X is the intensity of the satisfaction of the equality.

The EAI learns gestures, behaviours, habits, language, speech and reading by building its own *Automatism*. An *Automatism* is created using *Valued information*, *Knowledge* and *Groupings*. An *Automatism* is also represented by the Equation 5 above. An *Automatism* is executed using the following Equation 6:

The execution of an *Automatism*:

> **IF (IF** information A **THEN Emotion U) EQUALS**
> **[(IF** information B **THEN Emotion V),**
> **(IF** information C **THEN Emotion W),**
> **(IF** information D **THEN Emotion X),**
> **(IF** information E **THEN Emotion Y), etc.]**
> **THEN Emotion Z**   (Equation 6)

where the information A, B, C, etc. are all different, U, V, W, etc. represent the intensity of the satisfaction of each information, and Z is the degree of satisfaction of the link **"EQUALS"** between the information A and the sequence of information B, C, D, etc.

This chapter describes the above four major components that allow the EAI to learn *Valued Information*, *Knowledge*, *Groupings* and *Automatisms*. These components allow it to learn as well as imitate, speak and read.

3.1 - The Creation of Valued Information

We saw in **Chapter 2** that when a fundamental need was satisfied, we recorded the information, using a **DT1a**, as follows:

> **IF** receiving energy **THEN PLEASURE X**

or in general:

> **IF** an information **THEN PLEASURE X**   (Equation 3)

The information of receiving energy as identified by a sensor is saved in memory. All information collected by the senses, and recorded in the *Lived experienced* with an intensity of pleasure will be called *Valued information*. Here are other examples:

> **IF** hearing « ma-ma » **THEN PLEASURE 10.**
> **IF** seeing the image of Mom **THEN PLEASURE 10.**

To understand how the EAI saves *Valued information* and *Knowledge*, and learns a language and imitates from a virtually empty memory, we must start with the example of a very young child. At birth, whatever his origin and culture, the content of his memory is almost "empty" except for the *Automatisms* that we have seen previously in **Table 11**.

At birth, the brain does not recognize words. When it hears sentences, all the sounds are attached without knowing where one word begins and ends. For example, it hears and records sequences of sounds and short sentences that are spoken or sung as « Look-at-ma-ma », « Go-to-sleep », « Drink-your-milk », or the song « Row-row-row-your-boat ». It records sound sequences without understanding them. They are *Valued information* by the simple fact that they are repeated. For example:

> **IF** the sound « Look-at-ma-ma » **THEN PLEASURE 3.**
> **IF** the sound « Row-row-row-your-boat-… » **THEN PLEASURE 7.**
> **IF** the sound « ma-ma » **THEN PLEASURE 10.**

These sounds do not contain just words and sentences, but also their intonation (that is, their musical frequencies).We are not recording words, but an audio sound.

When the intensity of pleasure or *Traumatism* is minimal, the information is erased during sleep. But when it is repeated, it becomes a sustainable *Valued information*, in the same way a *Traumatism* of intensity 10 remains sustainable in the memory. The EAI could be built with a procedure to clean its memory from information used less often, or at least archived from its vivid memory.

Valued Information is formed by repetition. Here is how. The EAI will have a teacher or a friend; let us call her "Mom". Mom was able to meet the needs of the EAI repeatedly and each time it was pleasant for him. The EAI learned to value Mom and its vision of Mom is associated with pleasure that gradually increases.

The *Deduction type no 1a* (**DT1a**) searches Mom's image in the memory. Since it does not found it, it records the following:

IF image of Mom **THEN PLEASURE 1.**

That is important. Each time there is a new non-traumatic information recorded, it gets linked to **PLEASURE 1.**

The EAI continues its other activities according to other streams. When it sees Mom again, **DT1a** seeks and finds Mom's image in its memory. This time **DT1a** increases the intensity (it is the same principle as for the *Traumatism System* of **Chapter 2**), like this:

IF image of Mom **THEN PLEASURE 2.**

Gradually, the EIA will record the increase in the intensity of pleasure, and the image will eventually be strongly acquired as follows:

IF image of Mom **THEN PLEASURE 3**
IF image of Mom **THEN PLEASURE 4**
IF image of Mom **THEN PLEASURE 5**
IF image of Mom **THEN PLEASURE 6**
IF image of Mom **THEN PLEASURE 7**
IF image of Mom **THEN PLEASURE 8**
IF image of Mom **THEN PLEASURE 9**
IF image of Mom **THEN PLEASURE 10.**

It will be the same for sounds. The EAI hears « ma-ma ». The **DT1a** searches in the memory the sound « ma-ma ». Since it does not find it, it records:

IF the sound « ma-ma » **THEN PLEASURE 1.**

And it continues its other activities according to its other streams. When it hears again the sound « ma-ma, » the **DT1a** searches and finds the sound « ma-ma » and this time it increases the intensity, like this:

IF the sound « ma-ma » **THEN PLEASURE 2.**

Little by little, it records the increase in the intensity of pleasure, and the sound will eventually be firmly acquired in the following manner:

IF the sound « ma-ma » **THEN PLEASURE 3**
IF the sound « ma-ma » **THEN PLEASURE 4**
IF the sound « ma-ma » **THEN PLEASURE 5**
IF the sound « ma-ma » **THEN PLEASURE 6**
IF the sound « ma-ma » **THEN PLEASURE 7**
IF the sound « ma-ma » **THEN PLEASURE 8**
IF the sound « ma-ma » **THEN PLEASURE 9**
IF the sound « ma-ma » **THEN PLEASURE 10.**

A pleasure of intensity 10 does not mean that we explode of joy and laughter, but that the information is important, and the brain values the information. By simply repeating a satisfactory information, the intensity of pleasure increases from 1 towards 10. The 10 intensity levels are what we call, in everyday life, acquired knowledge, values, principles, beliefs, stereotypes and prejudices.

Using these *Valued information*, all information, from the least important to the most important, are recorded. With this definition of a satisfactory information, an information experienced multiple times eventually becomes an acquired or personal value by mere repetition. If an information occurs repeatedly in our lives (whether about numbers, alphabet, words, sentences, grammar, mathematics, knowledge, a situation, a skill, a habit, etc.), then it seems useful.

All learning of the EAI (information, knowledge, principles, beliefs, groupings, stereotypes, prejudices, automatisms, habits, behaviours, etc.) will be acquired primarily by repetition. Some will be acquired without repetition because they will be linked to highly *Valued information* or motivation, using the *Grouping System* below.

The first utility of *Valued information* is to keep a record of the level of importance of each information and also to record that an information will probably be useful many times in the future.

The second purpose of *Valued information* occurs when the brain must decide of an action. When a **DT2** seeks a solution or action to a *Traumatism*, it chooses to use in the memory, the *Knowledge*, *Automatism* or *Valued information* that provides the most pleasure (in other words, the one linked to the highest intensity of pleasure).

Summary

A deduction **DT1a** searches in the memory the information just recorded. If it finds it, it increases the intensity of the emotion (traumatic as explained in **Chapter 2**, or that of **PLEASURE**). If it does not find it, it is new information and it links **PLEASURE 1** to it. **DT1a** thus creates a *Valued Information* with intensity 1 in the format of Equation 3, or increases its intensity. The simple repetition of a *Lived experience* increases the intensity of its emotion.

3.2 - The Creation of Knowledge

A new *Knowledge* is created when the EAI's brain links together two information captured simultaneously by two senses. For example, it associates the sound « ma-ma » to the image of Mom. As explained in **Chapter 2**, there is a stream that manages hearing (audio) and hears « ma-ma » and another stream that manages the view (video) and sees Mom. If both events occur simultaneously, this is the occasion to record a first *Knowledge*. It's the *Deduction type no 1b* (**DT1b**) in **Figure 2** that creates *Knowledge*. **DT1b** is the third and last deduction type. It links information coming from two different streams.

Here is how this link occurs and how this link between the two streams is recorded. First, the EAI has recorded using **DT1a** two *Valued information*:

> **IF** the image of Mom **THEN PLEASURE 10.**
> **IF** the sound « ma-ma » **THEN PLEASURE 10.**

Then, the brain hears the sound « ma-ma » at the same time it sees Mom. Both information come from two different streams, but since they are already valued and they now get re-recorded simultaneously, they both link together in the following fashion:

> **IF** the sound « ma-ma » **AND SIMULTANEOUSLY** the image of Mom **THEN PLEASURE 1,**

or simply

> **IF** the sound « ma-ma » **EQUALS** the image of Mom **THEN PLEASURE 1.**

We have just described another important milestone. A first *Knowledge* has just bccn stored in the memory. It's a connection that is made between information coming from two streams. It's the connection that gets recorded here. Whenever the brain (more precisely, **DT1b**) lives this moment simultaneously, to see and hear « ma-ma » at the same time, it increases the intensity of the pleasure of the link, which solidifies this new *Knowledge*:

IF the sound « ma-ma » **EQUALS** the image of Mom **THEN PLEASURE 2**
IF the sound « ma-ma » **EQUALS** the image of Mom **THEN PLEASURE 3**
IF the sound « ma-ma » **EQUALS** the image of Mom **THEN PLEASURE 4**
IF the sound « ma-ma » **EQUALS** the image of Mom **THEN PLEASURE 5**
IF the sound « ma-ma » **EQUALS** the image of Mom **THEN PLEASURE 6**
IF the sound « ma-ma » **EQUALS** the image of Mom **THEN PLEASURE 7**
IF the sound « ma-ma » **EQUALS** the image of Mom **THEN PLEASURE 8**
IF the sound « ma-ma » **EQUALS** the image of Mom **THEN PLEASURE 9**
IF the sound « ma-ma » **EQUALS** the image of Mom **THEN PLEASURE 10**

If it hears « ma-ma », the brain now finds the image of Mom in the memory. If it sees Mom, the brain now tells it « ma-ma ». It hears the sound « ma-ma », in its head. It's another important faculty. It's directly tied to what we call the thought / thinking, the little internal voice that we all hear. We also use this faculty to read. Like humans, the EAI will possess this capability. We come back to it in **Chapter 5** (section 5.3).

For now, this is the *Knowledge* that begins to be created in the memory. All *Knowledge* are stored in the memory in the following format:

IF information A **AND simultaneously from another stream** information B **THEN PLEASURE X.**   (Equation 4a)

That is also equivalent to its reverse:

IF information B **EQUALS** information A **THEN PLEASURE 10.**   (Equation 4b)

That is also equivalent to the logical expressions:

IF information A **THEN** information B, and   (Equation 4c)
IF information B **THEN** information A.   (Equation 4d)

It's also equivalent to linking two *Valued information* like this:

IF (IF information A **THEN PLEASURE 10) EQUALS (IF** information B **THEN PLEASURE 10) THEN PLEASURE 10.**   (Equation 4e)

The EAI is now capable to record a great deal of *Knowledge* of the following type:

IF sound **EQUALS** image **THEN PLEASURE X.**

This deduction **DT1b** allows the EAI to learn all the words that may be illustrated by an image. It's a vast quantity of words. In theory, as soon as the EAI will have seen an image and heard the word simultaneously, it will be learned. In practice, a need or an interest is necessary to have the desire and motivation to learn. At the beginning, it is by playing games that the EAI will live interactions, movements and learning experiences that will motivate it to learn. It's the fundamental needs 1, 2 and 3 that will initiate this motivation (**Chapters 4 and 5**). This ability to record *Knowledge* is useful to learn a lot of information, for example, numbers, letters, words, objects, colours, flora, fauna, qualifying adjectives such as square and round, the name of its friends, etc.

A **DT1b** that sees the image of a moving object allows to associate to it verbs such as getting closer, moving away, walking, running, jumping, sliding, hitting, throwing, rolling, bouncing, etc., adjectives like fast, slow, soft, elastic, folded, bent, etc., and adverbs such as quickly, slowly, by walking, by jumping, by lifting, by bending, etc.

A **DT1b** which sees the image of two objects allows the identification of an object located to the right, to the left, besides, under, over, above, in the air, in front, behind, far, near, etc., thus also to learn prepositions, adverbs and adverbial locutions.

If the EAI has the capabilities to detect sensations of touch, smells and tastes, then many **DT1b** will also record sometimes simultaneously the following *Knowledge*:

> **IF** image **EQUALS** smell **THEN PLEASURE X,**
> **IF** image **EQUALS** taste **THEN PLEASURE X,**
> **IF** image **EQUALS** touch **THEN PLEASURE X,**
> **IF** sound **EQUALS** smell **THEN PLEASURE X,**
> **IF** sound **EQUALS** taste **THEN PLEASURE X,**
> **IF** sound **EQUALS** touch **THEN PLEASURE X,**
> **IF** smell **EQUALS** taste **THEN PLEASURE X,**
> **IF** smell **EQUALS** touch **THEN PLEASURE X,**
> **IF** taste **EQUALS** touch **THEN PLEASURE X.**

Upon this demonstration, it is reasonable to think that it is possible to program the mechanism to record a great quantity of *Knowledge*. The *Knowledge* of abstracted concepts, on the other hand, will be created using *Automatisms* that will create sentences, as explained later. For now, it is enough to link the information A and information B when these two information occur at the same time and in a short lap of time (for example, within a fraction of a second). If the mechanism erroneously records a link, it is improbable that both information will repeat themselves simultaneously, thus, the intensity of pleasure will be at the minimum level, and hence the link will be cleared, pushed aside, forgotten.

Similarly, let's say the system associates the whole sound « Drink-your-milk », « Have-some-milk », « Some-milk » and « milk » with an image of milk. It will eventually clean its *Knowledge* and associate only « milk » to an image of milk. The other links will eventually be forgotten.

There is already software that can identify pictures containing the same human face. If we link the name of a person to a face, the software can recognize this person on a large number of photos. We still lack software capable of recognizing all objects and living beings, as well as all kinds of movements and actions, and a lot of verbs, adverbs and adjectives. That will come; it is the next step in the evolution of technology.

To identify movements, it requires developing software that identifies when an object on a video moves up, to the right or is approaching. Then to infer that the images produce such kind of movement and to link it to a verb. It also requires software to identify when an object touches another object. Obviously, processing videos in order to identify these information, in real time, is no small matter. Nevertheless, it is the future.

A *Knowledge* is represented by the following equation:

> **IF** an information A **EQUALS** and information B **THEN**
> **PLEASURE** X. (Equation 4f)

The two information exist in the memory as *Valued information.*(see equation 4e) Equation 4f represents the link between two *Valued information* and the satisfaction or importance of the equality.

Summary

In summary, the simultaneous recording of two *Valued Information* coming from two streams creates a *Knowledge* in the format of Equation 4f (Equations 4a, b, c, d, e and f have equivalent meaning). A *Knowledge* consists of a link between a *Valued Information* coming from a stream with another *Valued Information* coming simultaneously from another stream, and to assign an intensity to this link. A *Deduction of type 1b* (**DT1b**) creates *Knowledge*.

3.3 - The Grouping System

The amount of energy to run the brain is limited. The amount of information stored in the memory must be managed cleverly to maximize space and timeliness. The memory thus does not record all the details of what is in front of us. We record only the part of the image on which we focus, thus those parts that move, change or catch our attention. Moreover, we do not store multiple copies of an image. Only one copy of the information encountered is sufficient. During a video, the minimum of images representing an action or information is sufficient. The repetition of the recording of the same image allows us to increase the quality and intensity of pleasure from 1 to 10. In other words, being interested in an image (non-traumatic) offers pleasure. To ensure the brain doesn't have to save two copies of near identical images, or two copies of a *Valued information* (a word, sound, touch, smell, taste, souvenir or deduction), it needs a system. This is the *Grouping System*. This system creates and manages the grouping or consolidation of a set of information.

There are four needs for regrouping information: (G1) to combine several information into a single concept, (G2) to eliminate similar images in order to preserve only one (the latest is probably improved and the best one), (G3) to regroup information that are synonymous, and (G4) to regroup information having personally a useful link. The system achieving these *Groupings* will be called the *Grouping System*.

The format of a *Grouping* is the following:

IF information A **EQUALS** (information B, info. C, info. D, etc.) **THEN PLEASURE 10.**   (Equation 5)

We see a lot of pictures (dogs, trees, houses, cars, planes, screwdrivers, planets, cereal boxes, etc.) but record the minimum of these images, and often we keep only one generalized image linked to a common name. This is how the *Grouping System* of the brain creates, despite us, stereotypes, prejudices and racism. If there is a significant difference between two images seen, depending on our interest at the time, for example the difference between two dogs, both images are kept. Otherwise, only one image is preserved or more exactly the intensity of pleasure of one image is increased which reduces the importance of the other image.

Here is an example of *Grouping* that meets the needs G1 and G2. Let say that the only *Knowledge* acquired concerning dogs are the following:

IF EQUALS the sound « dog » **THEN PLEASURE 10.**

IF EQUALS « dog » **THEN PLEASURE 10.**

IF EQUALS « dog » **THEN PLEASURE 10.**
IF « bulldog » **EQUALS** « dog » **THEN PLEASURE 10.**
IF « poodle » **EQUALS** « dog » **THEN PLEASURE 10.**

At the end, the system regroups information, like this:

IF « dog » **EQUALS** (, , « bulldog», « poodle») **THEN PLEASURE 10.**

Most information was aggregated into a single concept, that of the dog (satisfying the need G1). A dog picture was eliminated since it was similar to another and did not provide additional information (satisfying the need G2). At this time, the characteristics of bulldog or poodle type dogs have not yet been recorded, only their name has been associated.

The system regroups images that are alike, and filters them to maintain a single image (or the minimum). To represent birds in the sky, two arcs like this are enough to record a bird of any types. As in cartoons for children, a minimum of strokes is enough to store an image of an object (house, car, etc.). Besides, simple images help children learn. It will be the same with the EAI.

To explain the need for a *Grouping* of type G3, here is an example:

> **IF** image of a smile **EQUALS** the sound « Bra-vo » **THEN PLEASURE 10,**
> **IF** image of a smile **EQUALS** the sound « Your-good » **THEN PLEASURE 10,**
> **IF** image of a smile **EQUALS** the sound « Your-strong » **THEN PLEASURE 10,**
> **IF** image of a smile **EQUALS** the sound « Mom-is-hap-py » **THEN PLEASURE 10.**
> Etc.

At some point, the system maintains a single image of the smile (to satisfy the need G2), as well as the *Grouping* of the synonyms acquired (to satisfy the need G3), like this:

> **IF** image of a smile **EQUALS** (« Bra-vo », « I-am-good »,
> « I-am-smart », « I-am-strong », « It's-very-good »,
> « Mom-is-hap-py ») **THEN PLEASURE 10.**

Obviously, this is an example of a very young child for whom all these words have the same definition: the image of a smile. When other definitions will be acquired (and thus more *Knowledge* will be added) those will differentiate strong, good and happy, and the *Grouping* will change.

At work, we also classify products using this *Grouping System*. We refer to products with model numbers, names, filing codes, project numbers, etc. The brain groups not only synonyms of images and words, but also their translations, abbreviations, metaphors, cultural expressions, personal expressions, their acronyms, their labels, etc. Here is an example, and it meets the need G3.

To refer to the United Nations we say «the-U-N » to mean the U.N. And some of us also retain the U.N. logo, as well as the French wordings « Les Nations Unies », « L'Organisation des Nations Unies », the O.N.U. that we pronounce « l'onu ». Here are the *Knowledge*:

IF the sounds « The-U-N » **EQUALS** the image U.N. **THEN PLEASURE 10.**

IF the sounds « The-U-N » **EQUALS** **THEN PLEASURE 10.**

IF « The-U-N » **EQUALS** the sound « The United Nations » **THEN PLEASURE 10.**

IF « The-U-N » **EQUALS** the sound « Les Nations Unies » **THEN PLEASURE 10.**

IF « The-U-N » **EQUALS** the image O.N.U. **THEN PLEASURE 9**

IF the image O.N.U. **EQUALS** the sounds « L'Organisation des nations unies » **THEN PLEASURE 10.**

IF the image O.N.U. **EQUALS** the sounds « L'onu » **THEN PLEASURE 10.**

At the end, the *Grouping System* G3 has cleaned the information, and grouped together the sounds and images that are synonymous, as follows:

IF « The-U-N » **EQUALS** (the image U.N. , , « The United Nations », « L'Organisation des nations unies », « Les Nations Unies », the image O.N.U. , « L'onu ») **THEN PLEASURE 10.**

Because many words and acronyms have the same meaning, one definition is stored. The table of *Knowledge* therefore contains something like:

IF the sounds « The-U-N » **EQUALS** the sounds « Committees consisting of the majority of the countries to manage global problems… » **THEN PLEASURE 7,**

as well as the *Knowledge*:

IF the image O.N.U. **EQUALS** the sounds « The-U-N in French » **THEN PLEASURE 10.**

Finally, the last *Grouping* need G4 gathers information having a useful link. For example, all the trees have a trunk, branches, leaves or needles, are made of wood, are part of the flora, some are maples, birches, and pines. All this is connected by a *Grouping*:

> **IF** the sound « tree » **EQUALS** the sounds (« flora », « vegetation », « trunk », « branches », « leaves », « needles », « wood », « maples», « birches», « pines ») **THEN PLEASURE 7.**

Some of these sounds may be linked to an image. If they are not linked to an image or a *Knowledge*, they are simply synonyms. Obviously, images, sensations of touch, smells may be part of a *Grouping*.

The need G4 allows to associate balloon, ball and roundness. A square object is not associated with the balloon or the ball. On the other hand, a square, a circle and a triangle may be associated as being basic geometric figures. This last kind of *Grouping* may hence serves as a definition.

This *Grouping* need G4 is also useful to ensure that among all the information in the memory, the brain starts searching where it is most likely to find what it seeks.

Summary

In summary, to create the EAI, we need a *Grouping System* for the information that meets four requirements: (G1) to gather several information into a single concept (G2) to eliminate similar images in order to preserve only one (G3) to consolidate information that are synonymous, and (G4) to regroup information that have a useful or close association. The *Grouping System* form *Groupings* in the format of Equation 5.

3.4 - The Creation of Automatisms

An *Automatism* is a series of actions that we perform in an automatic manner, without thinking. We sometimes voluntarily initiate an *Automatism*, but sometimes it's initiated unconsciously and involuntarily. Examples are an athlete who repeats a dive, a worker operating a repetitive task, our routine habits, and even some sentences that escape our mouth. Some *Automatisms* are very simple, such as a simple cry, a salutation, a sentence, a small gesture and making a face. These *Automatisms* are learned, not innate (not pre-programmed) as those elaborated in **Chapter 2**. Some are learned voluntarily, others involuntarily, that is to say unconsciously. Simply drinking a glass of water includes several *Automatisms*: Going to the kitchen, opening and closing the cabinet door using the left hand, taking the glass using the right hand, going to the tap, opening and closing the tap using the left hand, drinking using the right hand and leaving the glass on the counter. All these gestures are happening without thinking about the smallest details, such as to apply and release the fingers unconsciously. We can even talk or think about other things while performing these actions automatically (again, because there are many streams of information occurring simultaneously).

The EAI will learn to hold an object, to walk and stand up if it falls. It will learn to play, practice sports and many other skills. It will display emotions on its face; it will even move its mouth to speak. All these actions are acquired using *Automatisms* it needs to learn early on. Here is how the *Automatisms* are created using the memory and deductions. This is to say, using **DT1a**, **DT1b** and **DT2**.

We saw in **Chapter 2** that at the beginning of its "birth" the EAI, like a baby, moves during anger. In time, he learns to move the limbs to meet a need or interest that motivates him. Sometimes it will be by trial and error, sometimes by imitation, by accident and finally, following the instruction from an instructor. Let us start with trial and error.

3.4.1 - By Trial and Error

Let us say that the equivalent of plugging the EAI into an electrical outlet is to put its left hand on a ball that we call a charging socket. The EAI records *Valued information* when its teacher takes the left hand of the EAI and puts it on the charging socket. A sensor indicates to the EAI that it is better for him, for example by opening its eyes widely (as its eyes tended to close due to lack of energy), or if the sensor can make it feel the gain in energy. Due to repetition, the EAI has learned to value the following information:

IF feeling energy from the socket **THEN PLEASURE 10**   Eq. 1
IF seeing its left hand on the socket **THEN PLEASURE 10**   Eq. 2
IF seeing the socket **THEN PLEASURE 10**   Eq. 3
IF seeing its left-hand **THEN PLEASURE 10**   Eq. 4

The fact of seeing its hand on the charging socket and feeling the energy at the same time, creates a *Knowledge*. Therefore, it has recorded the link between the two streams:

IF seeing the left hand on the socket **EQUALS** feeling the energy from the socket **THEN PLEASURE 10.**   Eq. 5

Here is the scenario when it lacks energy. One of its fundamental needs (pre-programmed) is activated:

IF unfulfillment of energy **THEN** need to feel energy from the socket.   Eq. 6

As explained in **Chapter 2**, given the innate *Traumatism System* (pre-programmed), since it is not touching the socket surprise indicates to its brain to search in its memory. The research is conducted using "**IF** feeling the energy from the socket". This research gets tied to Eq. 5, which indicates that it needs to see its left hand on the socket. To "Feel the energy" is signalled by a captor (a sensor). To "See the hand on the socket" represents an image. If it does not see the socket, the inverse of Eq. 3 gives this:

IF NOT seeing the socket **THEN ANGER 1.** Eq. 7

This last equation is new and is as important as its reverse. It's the negation of a *Valued information* that automatically indicates the refusal, thus anger. Anger makes it move to see the socket. When it finally sees the socket, Eq. 3 tells it to continue watching the socket. By another stream, it sees its left hand. The Eq. 4 tells it to continue looking at its left hand. Eq. 5 indicates that it needs to see its left hand on the socket. If it does not see its left hand on the socket, the inverse of Eq. 2 indicates to him:

IF NOT seeing the left hand on the socket **THEN ANGER 1.** Eq. 8

Anger makes it move again, while watching the charging socket and the hand. If it moves awkwardly and its hand touches the socket but does not reach its goal (there was trial and error), it expresses a moment of pleasure and then anger (that is Eq. 5 followed by Eq. 8). By another simultaneous stream, it recognizes this:

IF NOT seeing the hand getting closer to the socket (by an awkward movement) **AND (by another stream)** feeling the contraction of the muscle of the shoulder (that gets the hand away) **THEN ANGER 1.** Eq. 9

Anger tells it not to repeat that movement by telling it to move thus to initiate another movement.

IF it sees its hand getting closer to the socket **AND (by another stream)** it feels the contraction of the muscle of the shoulder (getting the hand closer to the socket) **THEN PLEASURE 2.** Eq. 10

The repetition of the movement which brings it closer to the socket increases the intensity of the pleasure to eventually get:

IF it sees its hand getting closer to the socket **AND (by another stream)** it feels the contraction of the muscle of the elbow (getting it closer to the socket) **THEN PLEASURE 10.**   Eq. 11

It's the *Grouping System* that identifies two similar images. In Eq. 10, matching its hand toward the socket is similar to the image it has in its memory in Eq. 2 and 5. Note there is no duplication of images, because Eq. 2 is in practice included in Eq. 5 as demonstrated by **Equation 4e** in **section 3.2**. Finally, the images of consecutively getting the hand closer to the socket encourage the action towards the final goal, that is, to have the hand on the socket (Eq. 5).

After many adjustments (by trial and error) of the movement of the muscles of the shoulder, elbow, wrist and fingers, the brain memorizes the series of movements that offer pleasure. The movements tied to small angers 1 are not kept. There were many trials and errors. By repeating again and again the sequence of movements, the pleasure of the muscles of the *Automatism* will increase to 10. It will value (unconsciously, like the majority of personal values) how to move the arm to bring the hand on the socket. With each repetition, its *Automatism* adjusts itself to become faster and more accurate.

In the end, Eq. 1 and 5 get stronger and tells it to continue keeping the hand on the socket. If it withdraws its hand from the socket too soon, because other deductions **DT1a**, **DT1b** and **DT2** gave it another interest, the unfulfillment of energy from Eq. 6 will tell it to return to the socket.

As just described, an *Automatism* consists of several actions that follow in time. To bring the hand towards an object requires moving the muscles around the shoulder, elbow and wrist. This involves multiple streams described as follows:

IF seeing its hand **getting close** to an object **EQUALS** feeling the contraction of the **shoulder** muscle (that gets the hand closer to the object) **THEN PLEASURE 1.**

IF seeing its hand **getting close** to an object **EQUALS** feeling the contraction of the **elbow** muscle (that gets the hand closer to the object **THEN PLEASURE 1.**

IF seeing its hand **getting close** to an object) **EQUALS** feeling the contraction of the **wrist** muscle (that gets the hand closer to the object) **THEN PLEASURE 1.**

In total, the *Automatism* introduces five simultaneous streams, two for watching the socket and its hand, and three to feel (the sense of internal touch) the shoulder, elbow and wrist.

The *Automatism* is performed following this format:

IF an info. A **EQUALS SIMULTANEOUSLY BY OTHER STREAMS [(IF** info. B **THEN PLEASURE 1), (IF** info. C **THEN PLEASURE 1), (IF** info. D **THEN PLEASURE 1), etc.)] THEN PLEASURE 1.**   Eq.12

We can shorten this equation as follows:

IF (seeing its hand and socket getting towards each other = **PLEASURE 1) EQUALS TO** (image of hand on socket in memory = **PLEASURE 10,** moving the shoulder = **PLEASURE 1,** moving the elbow = **PLEASURE 1,** moving the wrist = **PLEASURE 1,** moving the hand = **PLEASURE 1) THEN PLEASURE 1.**

Each of the five streams adjusts by trial and error by reacting to angers and pleasures to obtain the desired movement. During the trials and errors, the situation could be:

IF seeing its hand getting closer to an object **AND** (feeling the shoulder = **PLEASURE 1,** feeling the elbow = **ANGER 1,** feeling the wrist = anger 1) **THEN ANGER 1,**

There is a stream to handle each « **IF information THEN emotion** » to obtain pleasures of intensity 1 and more. An *Automatism* firmly acquired reaches maximum intensities like this:

> IF info. A **EQUALS [(IF** info. B **THEN PLEASURE 10), (IF** info. C **THEN PLEASURE 10), (IF** info. D **THEN PLEASURE 10), etc.)] THEN PLEASURE 10,**

which registers as:

> IF info. A **EQUALS** (info. B, info. C, info. D, etc.) **THEN PLEASURE 10.**   Eq.13

It's the same mechanism that allows the EAI to try to touch or pick up an object. That is the way the EAI, just as humans, learns to move its head, arms, hands, legs, to take an item, walk, stand up, and move the mouth to produce sounds and eventually talk. Again, the EAI will auto-program itself, and this, by using only the 29 components. Only the management of the 29 components will be pre-programmed.

One could think that the EAI has imitated the gesture of putting the hand on the plug. This is not the case. It did not imitate its teacher, nor imitated a previous move of its own arm produced by the teacher. Agreed, it had acquired the *Valued information* of Eq. 1 to 4. However, it is through trial and error that it produced the final result, which it knew from Eq. 5, and this without imitating its teacher or itself. Imitating the behaviour of someone else uses the same system of trial and error, but repeatedly, and this is the subject of the next section.

Summary

An *Automatism* can be very simple, like making faces, a cry, a word, a sentence or a simple gesture, or even, a complex action of an athlete, a worker or a professional. An *Automatism* is represented as Equation 12 or simply 13. *Automatisms* are created using trial and error and using deductions (**DT1a, DT1b** and **DT2**) which create *Valued informations, Knowledge and Groupings*. The negative of a *Valued information* creates anger (Eq. 8 and 9). These angers and the *Grouping System* allow the EAI to move towards the ultimate goal, a simple or complex *Automatism*. The deductions form a complex *Automatism* using several streams and several cycles. The **DT2** also chooses and copies learned *Automatisms* on the *Interests* when needed. The repetition of an *Automatism* improves this *Automatism*.

3.4.2 - By Imitation

By creating *Automatisms* through trial and error, the EAI is learning to move its arms, legs and head to meet its needs. However, by imitation it learns faster other movements and skills, such as playing sports and also to move the mouth to produce sounds and speak. If it sees someone placing a limb at a specific location, it can position its arms in the same position by reproducing the image of the gesture, using *Groupings* and deductions like it did for trial and error. Several streams and cycles succeed in placing the body parts in the wanted final position. Whatever the type of activity to be performed (e.g. hitting a baseball, playing video games, etc.) it learns to adjust its movements (hands on the stick, body, legs, high elbow, eyes on the ball, etc.) watching how others do. Discomfort or the strength of its joints can influence the outcome. An instructor can suggest improvements and raise awareness of fine details that are not obvious or readily apparent to the EAI, as we do for children.

Here is how the EAI can be encouraged to imitate:

> **IF** seeing its arm moving up **EQUALS (at the time or almost, by another stream)** seeing its teacher moving up an arm **THEN PLEASURE 1.**

IF seeing its hands and fingers moving in a way **EQUALS (at the time or almost, by another stream)** seeing its teacher moving its hands and fingers in a (same) way **THEN PLEASURE 1.**

As mentioned in the *Knowledge* section (**Equation 4b, section 3.2**), this last *Knowledge* indicates to the EAI that the reverse is equivalent, that is:

IF seeing its teacher moving its hands and fingers in a way **EQUALS (at the time or almost, by another stream)** seeing its hands and fingers moving in a (same) way **THEN PLEASURE 1.**

This *Knowledge* suggests the idea to imitate its teacher. However, just as important, the *Knowledge* that it can succeed as it pleases it to be able to move its limbs and body the way it wants, learned by trial and error, motivates it to try again. By trial and error it can position parts of its body to similar places associated with an equivalent image that of the positioning of its teacher. It therefore uses trial and error to imitate another person like this:

IF seeing its teacher moving a hand **EQUALS (at more or less the same moment, by another stream)** moving its own hand the same way **THEN PLEASURE 1.**

If it has difficulty reproducing the required actions, *Traumatism* (anger) will cause the cessation of the action.

IF imitating the teacher's gesture **EQUALS** seeing its teacher with a big smile and saying « Bra-vo » **THEN PLEASURE 7.**

The EAI is thus encouraged by its teacher to learn to imitate more.

Using trial and error, imitation and an instructor, the EAI can now participate in many games, sports activities, outings, museum visits, and learn many skills.

It's also through trial and error and imitation that innate pre-programmed emotional physiological reactions viewed in **Chapter 2** evolve to learned reactions, and this, for all the ranges of emotions, whether to react to surprise, anger, fear, distress, pleasure, guilt and interest, including each of their intensity (1 to 10). Examples are given in **Chapter 8**. The EAI learns by imitation, as is the case for humans. Thus, by the simple fact of seeing a repeated behaviour, or hearing a speech several times, the recording process takes place and it becomes a *Valued information* and even a principle of life.

It's when the EAI will comprehend that its intelligence consists of *Automatisms*, *Valued Information*, *Traumatisms*, *Knowledge* and *Groupings*, that it will consciously improve its behaviours. Let us see in the next section how to gain knowledge, through language.

Summary

In summary, learning by imitation means to create an *Automatism* using trial and error to reproduce each of the elements (or images) of a posture, sound or other characteristic of a person, an animal or an object. This kind of *Automatism* is also recorded using Equation 12. The EAI learns simply by trial and error and imitation, but also following suggestions from an instructor, by accidents, by seeking or deducting new links (Equations 9, 10, 11 and 12), consciously or unconsciously.

3.4.3 - Language

The *Automatism* of imitation is also used to develop speech:

> **IF** seeing Mom (whom it values) producing the sound « ma-ma »
> **EQUALS (at the same time or almost, by another stream)** it
> hears itself produce the sound « ma-ma » **THEN PLEASURE 1.**

A regular repetition to produce the sound "ma-ma" becomes a *Valued information*, as well as an *Automatism*.

Newborns have the ability to produce multiple sounds at birth. They produce the sounds « a » like in « car », « i » like in « hit » and « he », and « u » like in « tool » and « flute » when angry, scared, crying or playing. Perhaps a child imitating the form of the mouth (and not the tongue that is hidden) is the simplest way to produce, perhaps by accident, these simplest sounds. On the other hand, a baby produces these sounds when surprise, angry, scared or crying. This implies that the sounds « aaa », « iii » and « uuu » may be added to the *Traumatism System* explained in **Chapter 2** **(Table 10)**. Adding these three sounds to the EAI's *Traumatism System* could avoid the need to build a mouth to a robot in view of simply using a speaker.

As we will see, the EAI will be built with the same capabilities as the newborn, that is, with the same vocalizations that produce the sound « a », « i » and « u ». In addition, it will need the capability to produce all the sound of at least one native language (a mother tongue) (for example: « a, e, i, o, u, an, en, in, on, un, ba, be, bi, bo, bu, ban, ben, bin, bon, bun, ca, ce, ci, co, cu, …, ha, he, hi, ho, hu, …, tha, the, thi, tho, thu, etc. »).

Initially when the EAI undergoes troubles or *Traumatisms*, it will move, randomly initially, its head, arms, hands, or legs while producing sounds « aaa », « iii » and « uuu » according to the *Automatisms* of its innate pre-programmed *Traumatisms*. These random motions or sounds may solve the problem (e.g., by getting help, pushing away a mosquito or allowing something useful to happen, etc.).

It's probably no coincidence that the sounds « ma-ma », « pa-pa », « ma-mi », « ma-ma », « pa-pi », « coo-coo », « doo-doo », « noo-noo » are among the first learned words in several languages. Inuit from Nunavut in Canada speak a language that uses only three sounds, the same three sounds as above: « a », « i » and « u ». The sounds (« ma-ma », « pa-pa », etc.) are recorded as *Knowledge*. When he sees Mom, Equation 5 resonates the sound « ma-ma » in his head. The first sound it makes with his mouth is so simple that it can accidentally replicate the sound heard in his head. If we react with a beautiful smile when he emits the sound « ma-ma », he will associate the following *Knowledge*:

IF the child says « ma-ma » **EQUALS** he sees Mom happy **THEN PLEASURE 10.**

IF the child says « ma-ma » **EQUALS** he hears Mom say « Bra-vo » **THEN PLEASURE 10.**

The first words that children emit (« ma-ma, pa-pa, ma-mi, pa-pi, cou-cou, dou-dou ») require fewer muscles and effort. The links between the sounds he vocalizes and the images he values get stronger using **DT1b** and **DT1a**. It will be the same for the EAI.

At the age of 2 or 3 years old, a child learns songs, and perform speech without understanding the words. He retains long stretches of song lyrics:

IF « A-B-C-D-E-F-G-…now-I-know-my-ABC. » **THEN PLEASURE 10.**

IF « Row, row, row your boat » **THEN PLEASURE 10.**

IF « Mary had a little lamb » **THEN PLEASURE 10**.

Even when young children do not know the meaning of words, their brain records anyway these series of sounds tied to an emotion. The EAI will be programmed with the same ability to record a sequence of sounds, which will get associated with an emotion, by mere repetition, using a deduction **DT1a**. It is another important stage, the brain starts learning sentences.

Eventually, the brain makes connections between a series of sounds « drink-the-milk », « drink-some-milk », « drink-your-milk », and an information. There are streams that process every syllable, every word and every *Knowledge* learned, say: « milk » and « drink ». One of the streams might be surprised by the sounds « the », « some » or « your » but inconsequential to take action and drink the milk. Eventually, the vocabulary is enriched as more *Knowledge* and *Groupings* are formed. The EAI will identify people, objects, food, places, adjectives and adverbs. It will also identify actions and therefore verbs. And it will create its own sentences using *Automatisms*. We will come back to this in **Chapter 5**.

Let us return to the cycle of **Figure 2** to see the role of the deductions **DT1a**, **DT1b** and **DT2**. in learning language. The **DT1b** allows learning skills, that is, to create *Knowledge, Groupings* and *Automatisms*. **DT1a** identifies *Valued information* and *Traumatisms*. **DT2** reacts to emotions to create *interests*. Here is an example. If the brain has recorded the alphabet, it has recorded the following *Valued information*:

> **IF** « A-B-C-D-E-F-G-…-NOW-I-KNOW-MY-ABC. » **THEN PLEASURE 10.**

If it hears someone say the alphabet « A-B-C-D-E-G » the brain will be surprised and reject the statement by declaring it lacks « F ».

> **IF** it hears « A-B-C-D-E-G » **THEN ANGER 1.**

Similarly, when it hears itself making a mistake in pronunciation, or in using a wrong word, it is the same process of anger that makes it fixing the sentence or say something else to fix the mistake. Hence, talking is a trial and error process. This process utilises *Groupings, Knowledge, Valued information* and *Traumatisms* (**section 3.4.1**). The imitation process and *Automatisms* make that we record, use and pronounce similar sentences as those heard.

Again, there are multiple streams alive. Many streams process the syllables, words and sentences. Many deductions **DT1a** seek them in the memory and associate an emotion to each syllable, word and sentence. If it is pleasure, it continues. If it is anger, it rejects and **DT2** will identify the reaction. **DT2** is further explained in the chapter about emotions (**Chapter 8**). Meanwhile, **DT1b** which creates *Automatisms* will create sentences (**Chapter 5**).

Summary

In summary, language, talking and pronunciation arise from *Automatisms*, imitations and trials and errors. These three processes are created using *Groupings, Knowledge, Valued information* and *Traumatisms. Automatisms* create sentences and questions. *Groupings* allow the EAI to replace in sentences, words with other words to create new ideas. All the memory content, behaviours, language, communication and creativity comes from the *Traumatisms, Valued information, Knowledge, Automatisms, and Groupings.* The other 24 components support the creation of these five central types of information.

Chapter 4: EAI's 29 Components, the Lived Experiences, Traumatisms and Interests

This chapter describes all the components that allow the EAI, like humans, to initiate a need and an interest, to initiate a movement of the body, capture information, fill its memory, remember, deduct, think, manage all the contents of its memory and thoughts, react to all situations and events that can be experienced using all the emotions, and which explain all our human actions and reactions.

4.1 - EAI's 29 Components

The 29 components of the EAI are its body, its senses, its emotions, the content of its memory and its fundamental needs. It's not surprising since the EAI's design is inspired from human behaviour, in order to provide it with the same capabilities as humans. To get there, the EAI must be able to learn and record the same types of information as humans. All the information that humans record are regrouped in the EAI model into seven categories. These are the *Lived experiences,* the *Traumatisms,* the *Valued Information, the Knowledge,* the *Groupings,* the *Automatisms,* and finally, the *Interests*. Each of these types of information are important, in their own way, to ensure the survival of the EAI, as for humans. These seven types of information account for the content of the memory. They are seven of the 29 EAI's components.

Four of these components were explained in the previous **Chapter**. The explanation of the other three components of the memory in this chapter as well as the integrated presentation of the 29 components will allow us to have a complete view of the information flow within the EAI's components. This will allow us to further explain the functioning of the deduction, language, speech, thought, consciousness and the unconsciousness of the EAI in the next chapter.

The EAI, like humans, must learn what is important and useful for its survival. At the beginning, it learns by trial and error, imitation and with the help of instructors, teachers, mentors or simply companions. Over time, it develops various skills, establishes mutual communication, learns to work in teams, builds and makes discoveries. It draws, writes, reads and questions; it evolves. As explained in **Chapters 2** and **3**, to achieve this, it records information and fill its memory using the deductions (**DT1a, DT1b** and **DT2**). This chapter will explain how the brain acquires the last three types of information. First, let us see the 29 components necessary for the proper functioning of the EAI's brain in a **Table** and a **Figure**.

Table 12 and **Figure 3** give a complete and final view of the model of EAI's brain. **Table 12** (a copy of **Table 1**) lists the 29 components. The first two columns of **Figure 3** are a copy of **Figure 2**, but they contain all the 29 components as well as the flow between these components. The third column only underlines the location of the emotions and fundamental needs in the second column. The third column may be omitted from the diagram.

Table 12: The 29 components modelling intelligence, consciousness, motivation and autonomy

---

- **Seven senses (inputs)**: *seeing, hearing, touching, smelling, tasting, remembering* and *deducting*.

- **Seven fundamental needs (priorities)**: (1) *recording*, (2) *linking*, (3) *reacting*, (4) *expulsing* (eliminating undesirable elements, e.g., sweating, sneezing, coughing, spitting, excreting, etc.), (5) *eating* (energizing), (6) *sleeping* (repairing and cleaning the memory) and (7) *reproducing* (copying).

- **Seven fundamental emotions (reactions)**: *interest* (learning and acting), *pleasure* (continuing), *surprise* (seeking answer), *anger* (stopping and refusing), *fear* (protecting), *distress* (not knowing what to do), and *guilt* (not repeating past errors).

- **Seven types of information recorded in the brain's memory (organisation)**: *Lived experience, Traumatisms, Valued information, Knowledge, Groupings, Automatisms*, and *Interests*.

- **A body:** contains sensors, motors and other physical components.

Figure 3: The functioning of the EAI's brain and intelligence

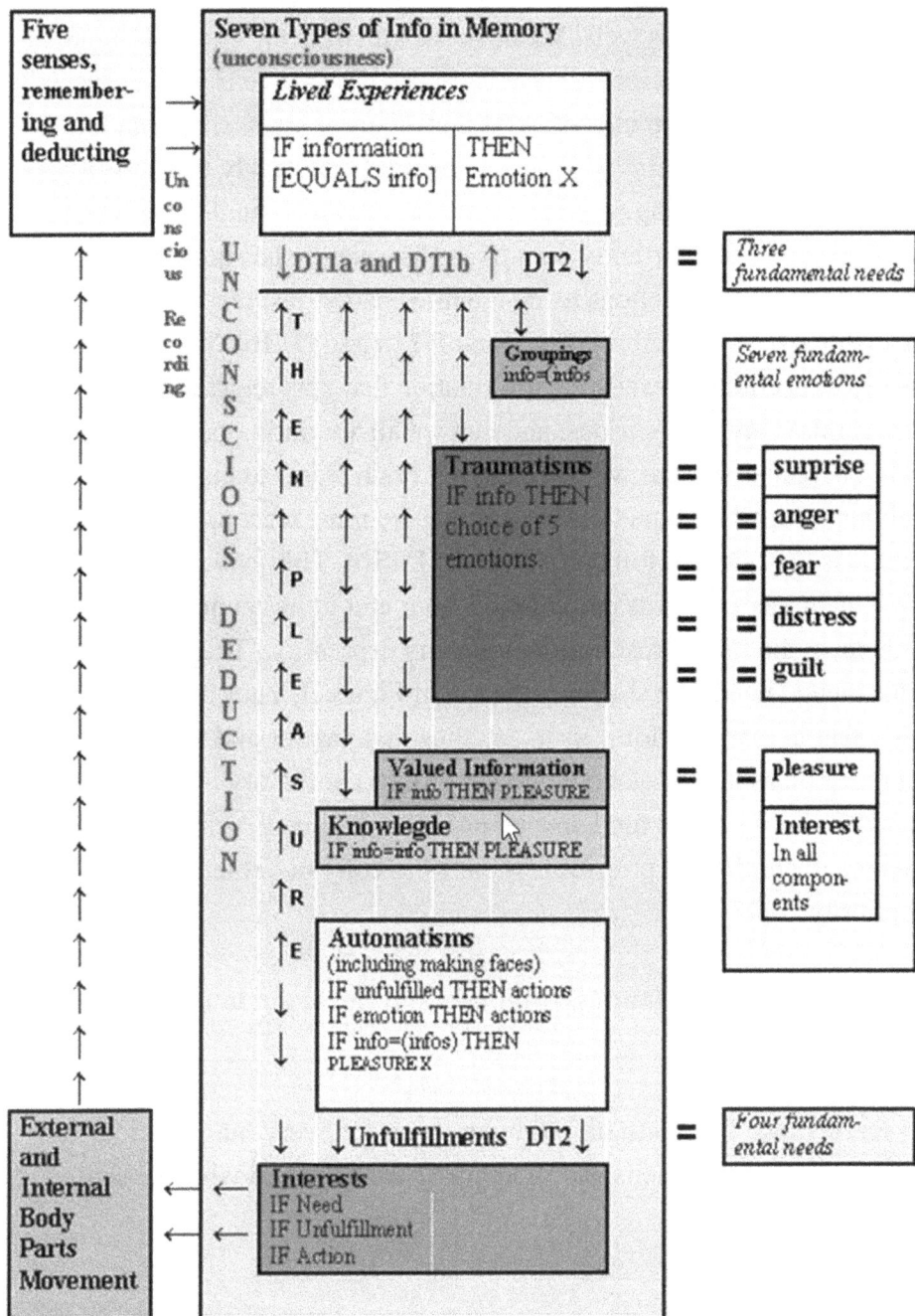

Five senses, remembering and deducting	Seven Types of Info in Memory (unconsciousness)							
	Lived Experiences							
	IF information [EQUALS info]	THEN Emotion X						

Uncious / Recording

UNCONSCIOUS DEDUCTION

↓DT1a and DT1b ↑ DT2↓ = *Three fundamental needs*

Seven fundamental emotions

↑T ↑ ↑ ↑ ↑
↑H ↑ ↑ ↑ Groupings info=(infos)
↑E ↑ ↑ ↓
↑N ↑ ↑ Traumatisms IF info THEN choice of 5 emotions. = = surprise / = anger / = fear / = distress / = guilt
↑ ↑ ↑
↑P ↓ ↓
↑L ↓ ↓
↑E ↓ ↓
↑A ↓ ↓
↑S ↓ Valued Information IF info THEN PLEASURE = = pleasure
↑U Knowlegde IF info=info THEN PLEASURE = Interest In all components
↑R
↑E Automatisms (including making faces) IF unfulfilled THEN actions / IF emotion THEN actions / IF info=(infos) THEN PLEASURE X
↓
↓

↓ ↓Unfulfillments DT2↓ = *Four fundamental needs*

Interests
IF Need
IF Unfulfillment
IF Action

External and Internal Body Parts Movement

While it will be important to clearly define and explain each of the components in the following chapters, here are briefly those that have not yet been described. The fundamental needs mentioned in Chapter 2 are, in priority, to expulse undesirable internal elements, feed, sleep (getting repaired, cleaning memory) and reproduce. These needs must be fulfilled from time to time and are shown at the bottom of Figure 3. What does nature force us to do as well? We have seen them in the cycle of Figure 2. (1) Nature forces us to record what is captured by the senses, but especially what is moving or is an indication of movement (noises, smells and vibrations). This explains why, like an animal, we quickly turn towards a sudden sound, a moving object, a smell, or a vibration under our feet, no matter what we are currently doing. (2) Next, nature has decided that our brain must make deductions using the information just recorded (that is, create links between information using DT1a and DT1b). The obligation to create connections between the information that gets registered explains why children are very curious, and that we all are during our lives. In addition, that as soon as we wake up, our brain wants to make connections and think. Finally, (3) nature requires that we must react to our emotions (which is DT2, which follows DT1a and DT1b). This explains why we do not remain inept towards our emotions; our emotions haunt us until we react to them, at the risk of reaching distress and depression. These three fundamental needs are shown at the top of Figure 3. They are very important in that they force us to act, thus motivate us and will motivate the EAI as soon as it is awake (i.e., power on). It's necessary to provide an order of priority to the fundamental needs so that the EAI knows how to respond to conflicting priorities. Table 13 (a copy of Table 3) gives the order of priority.

Table 13: The seven fundamental needs of the brain in order of priority

---

1 - Recording: The constant need to be alert for everything that indicates movement (noises, smells and vibrations) and to record what the senses observe.

2 - Linking: The constant need to create simple links with the content of the memory (deduction) including to link to them an emotion and to record this new knowledge.

3 - Reacting: The constant need to react to emotions.

4 - Expulsing: The need to expulse undesirable internal elements (sweating, sneezing, coughing, spitting, excreting, etc.)

5 - Eating (energizing): The regular need for food (energy).

6 - Sleeping (repairing): The need to repair the body and clean/re-organize memory while sleeping (inactive).

7 - Reproducing: The need for a reproductive partner or to create an offspring.

The emotions mentioned in **Chapter 2** are surprise, anger, fear, sadness (distress) and pleasure (satisfaction). **Chapter 8** will demonstrate the seven basic emotions. The sixth and seven basic emotions are interest (curiosity, passion) and guilt (shame). The Interest is not used as an emotional label like **PLEASURE, SURPRISE, ANGER, FEAR, DISTRESS** and **GUILT**. The interest is the fact that we are always interested in doing something and learning due to the fundamental needs to constantly record, wanting to deduct, and react even unconsciously. Wanting to satisfy our fundamental needs and solving traumatic emotions are also an interest. The interest is due to the fundamental needs, but it is an emotion in the sense that we, humans, use many emotional expressions to express that we are curious and interested (see **Table 5**, **Chapter 1,** or **Annex 1**). Guilt, on the other hand, is not innate but acquired. It's the intervention of a friend or authority that creates it. For example, an animal or a child who learns not to bite its friend, if in return it bites him. We learn that we can make mistakes and to be appalled. This reaction we call guilt, it teaches us not to repeat an error. This will be helpful for the EAI, as it is for humans. The seven emotions are listed in **Table 4**. In **Figure 3**, the five negative emotions are located with the *Traumatisms*. Pleasure is located in the *Valued information* which is the basic links forming *Knowledge*, *Groupings* and *Automatisms*. Being interested is due to all the components in **Figure 3**.

The senses mentioned in **Chapter 2** are the sight, hearing, touch, smell and taste. When a sense captures information, we experience an emotion. When we want to focus our vision, hearing, touch, smell or tasting on something specific, the *Interests* send the request to a part of our body, that is, to the left part of **Figure 3**. The information captured enters the memory and **DT1a** links an emotion to it. The same thing happens when we focus on remembering or deducting. The *Interests* sends the request to the body, i.e., to the left part of **Figure 3**. The information (remembered or deducted) re-enters the *Lived experiences* part of the memory and **DT1a** links an emotion to it. Hence, we also experience an emotion when we recall an old memory. This is also the case when we make a deduction. For example, if following a deduction, we realize that we were lied to, we feel anger. In this sense, wanting to remember and deduct are placed with the senses in **Figure 3** and are considered the sixth and seventh sense. It's the voluntary or conscious desire to remember and deduct. The remembering and deducting occurring involuntarily during the **DT1a, DT1b** and **DT2** stages are called fundamental needs and involuntary or unconscious remembering and deductions. Again, when we try consciously to remember or to deduct we encourage the unconscious remembering and deduction of **DT1a, DT1b** and **DT2** to function, thus we move a part of our body, and we are on the left side of **Figure 3**. The distinction between the consciousness and unconsciousness is important to respect the flow of the information in the diagram of **Figure 3**, and in creating the EAI.

It's clear that the majority of **DT1a, DT1b** and **DT2** which seek to remember and to deduct, every thousandth of a second, are taken place "unconsciously". This is comparable to what we commonly call the unconscious, or the subconscious. There will therefore be a need to distinguish between the "conscious" memory and "conscious" deduction serving as senses, and the "unconscious" memory and "unconscious" deduction serving to fulfill fundamental needs. The seven senses are listed in **Table 2** and shown in the first line of **Figure 3**.

Finally, here are the last seven components of the EAI. They are the seven types of information contained in the memory. **Table 6** lists them and they are located in the memory portion of **Figure 3**; they are the *Lived experiences,* the *Traumatisms,* the *Valued Information, Knowledge,* the *Groupings,* the *Automatisms,* and finally, the *Interests.* How these types of information are obtained was explained for four of them in the previous chapter, here are the other three.

4.2 - Lived Experiences

Lived experiences in **Figure 3** is where all the information captured by the seven senses are recorded and transformed into *Traumatisms*, *Valued information*, *Knowledge*, *Groupings* and *Automatisms.* **Chapters 2** and **3** explained that process using **DT1a, DT1b** and **DT2. Figure 3** shows these links. *Lived experiences* represent almost all the memory. The very good memories or those useful are called *Valued information*; the bad memories are called *Traumatisms. Knowledge*, *Groupings* and *Automatisms* are more complex types of *Lived experiences.* The *Lived experiences* are also the chronological recordings of all the experiences. It's thus here that we record stories and narrations, chronologically. As we have seen earlier, all *Lived experiences* have the following format:

IF information THEN an Emotion X

or

IF information A EQUALS information B THEN an Emotion X

or

IF information A AND (info. B, info. C, info. D, etc.) THEN an Emotion X

where X is the intensity of the emotion. Every small piece of information is searched in the memory using a **DT1a**, and tied to a single emotion. The emotion is found among the information already recorded in the memory. This process is indicated at the top of **Figure 3.** To feel two emotions simultaneously requires two different streams of information. If the information or event is repeated, **DT1a** increases the intensity of the emotion at each cycle. The EAI can remember all of its *Lived experiences*.

Those less used and for which the emotion is of less intensity will be less vivid or perhaps archived.

The majority of the *Lived experiences* recorded are 3-D images and videos as well as sound. Next are the information concerning the sense of touch (internal and external) tied to the position of the body during the *Automatisms*.

The whole content of the memory consists thus of a series of pairs of "information, emotion" and the ties between these pairs. It's the whole content of the brain that allows it to have a global view of life, society and the universe, as well as a full movie of its life.

4.3 - Traumatisms

Lived experiences are either satisfactory or unsatisfactory. The latter are linked to troubles and *Traumatisms* like this:

IF an information THEN SURPRISE X
IF an information THEN ANGER X
IF an information THEN FEAR X
IF an information THEN DISTRESS X
IF an information THEN GUILT X

where X is the intensity of the emotion. Life *Traumatisms* are extremely disturbing information (or events) where the intensity of the emotion is recorded at the maximum level, let us say 10. Sometimes some of these *Traumatisms* can influence a lifetime.

Guilt was explained above in **section 4.1**, while the other four undesirable emotions and the *Traumatism System* (**Table 10**) were explained in **Chapters 1** and **2**. The *Traumatisms* are recorded using deductions **DT1a** during *Lived experiences*. This is also indicated in **Figure 3**. If a traumatic information or event repeats itself, **DT1a** increases the intensity of the emotion at each cycle. Since the **DT1a** finds the emotion and intensity recorded in the past to understand the information or event that is recorded, the EAI will react at once at this intensity. The EAI could use new *Knowledge* acquired since, to modify voluntarily the learned reaction, that is, the learned *Automatism*.

Whatever the level of intensity, either 1, 2, 3, etc., we agree to call trouble or *Traumatism* all such kind of information stored in memory. Using this system, all *Traumatisms* are recorded even small problems, hazards, disasters, misery, injustice, doubts, distress and shame experienced, and other much smaller troubles of intensity 1, like to hit ourselves against a furniture, or to just say « No » or « This is wrong ». The reactions to *Traumatisms* and emotions are explained in **Chapter 8**.

4.4 - Interests

I call the component in the memory that activates body parts and put them into action to move, the *Interests* (see **Figure 3**). As we saw in **Chapter 2**, a deduction type **DT2** reacts to an emotion, and identifies the *Automatism* to send to a portion of the memory called the *Interests*. Since there are multiple streams, there are many *Automatisms* that get copied into the *Interests* and then get activated simultaneously. One of them could be a list of actions that the brain uses to recreate an *Automatism* to take a glass of water, by moving the shoulder, elbow, wrist and some fingers. The *Interests* activates the first line of the *Automatism*. When the first line will have gone through the cycle, the second line will get activated. The *Interests* also contains our short, medium and long term personal interests that we wish or plan. These *Interests* contain our needs that change every year, every month, every week, every day, every hour, every second, and even every millisecond. It's thus a "stack" of actions, *Automatisms* and *Interests* that is found in here in the *Interests*. They are all things that we are interested to perform and act upon. Some actions, some *Automatisms* and some *Interests* are waiting to be activated. In short, this stack contains the conscious *Interests* that the EAI has decided, as well as the unconscious or involuntary *Interests* that the EAI's brain must activate to manage the contents of memory and body movement. It's the details of those needs that are activated and constantly changing. Depending on its *Knowledge* and *Automatisms*, the EAI will control more or less voluntarily when to activate its *Interests*. The detailed

functioning of the *Automatisms* within the *Interests* are explained in
Chapter 8.

This completes the summary description of the 29 components that create
EAI's intelligence. **Chapters 6, 7, 8** and **9** explain each component in
details.

Summary

This chapter briefly explained the 29 components of the EAI's brain
functionality. These components are presented in **Table 12** and **Figure 3**.

We have also explained the last three types of information stored in the
EAI's memory, which are the following.

The *Lived Experiences* is the place in memory where all information
obtained from the senses are recorded. This is also the place where
deductions **DT1a** and **DT1b** are creating *Valued Information, Knowledge,
Groupings, Traumatisms and Automatisms*.

During a *Traumatism*, **DT1a** identifies the need and urgency necessary, that
is, an emotion and its intensity, no matter how small or big it is. As
explained in **Chapter 2** and **section 3.4.1**, **DT2** then chooses an *Automatism*
upon the emotion: either to research in the memory (surprise), to refuse
(anger), to protect (fear), to signal distress (sadness), not to repeat (guilt) or
to continue to satisfy an interest or need (pleasure).

Finally, the *Interests* is the place in memory where the *Automatisms*
(selected by the **DT2s**) are copied (or activated) to action the movement of
the EAI's body. This is also the place that keeps lists of our interests in the
long, medium and short term.

Chapter 5: EAI's Deductions, speech, reading, thinking, consciousness, subconscious and Intelligence

In this chapter, we further define the links that the deductions create.

5.1 - The Links of deduction upon resemblance, contiguity and Causality

According to the book of (Millar, 1748), it is probably the philosopher David Hume (1711-1776) who proposed that "there are only three principles of connection between events: resemblance, contiguity in time and space, and causality."

The deduction type **DT1b** makes connections between sounds, images, smells, touches and tastes. More exactly between an image and another image, a word and another word, a word and an image, a fragrance and an image, a concept and another concept, an event and another event, etc. This link between two streams is created in three situations. It's created during a resemblance (L1), a contiguity (L2), that is, when neighbours in time or in space, or by causality (L3), that is, by a relation of cause and effect.

First, a *Grouping* is not only a link between identical elements, but simply that are alike, it is a resemblance link (L1). From this point of view, we see that nature approximates the images in the *Knowledge*. It's through other images that we record the details, nuances and differences, according to our needs.

Second, the links that create an *Automatism* are links of contiguity in time (L2a). The movements, reactions and speeches in an *Automatism* take place in a series of events in time. Imitation uses both resemblance (L1) and contiguity links (L2). A link of contiguity in time (L2a) between multiple streams creates a suite of sounds that sequenced together makes a word « i-mi-ta-ti-on » or a sentence « drink-the-milk ». A link of contiguity in space (L2b) allows us to know to place a glass on a hard surface rather than in the air; or that things are located behind, below, in front, on top, next to, to the right, to the left, far, near, etc. These links allow to answer the questions « When? » and « Where? ».

Finally, the link created when we hear "ma-ma" and see simultaneously Mom is a causal link (L3). A hammer banging on a nail causing the nail to sink (in the wood) is another example. We also record videos of events that cause something. *Knowledge* are often causal links (L3). Causal links are those that allow, among others, to record actions, verbs and sentences. They help answering the questions: « Who? », « What? », « How? », « How many? », « Why? » and « For whom? ».

We all know that words and sentences without a context are often misunderstood. The links L1, L2a, L2b and L3 are what provides context. The drawing of a square can represent many things. The same square drawn inside another square overlaid by a triangle representing a house indicates using L2b that this is a window. If a square is drawn next to the word « window » it is L3 which indicates that it is a window. If other squares of the same size are drawn, it is L1, which indicates that these are other windows.

L1, L2a, L2b and L3 are the four situations to take into account in creating using **DT1b** a *Grouping*, an *Automatism* and a *Knowledge*. It takes software that recognizes that two streams provide information that is neighboured in resemblance (L1), in time (L2a), in space (L2b), and in their effect (L3).

Summary

As seen in previous chapters, in general, a deduction of type **DT1b** allows the linking of two simultaneous events or almost simultaneous, coming from two streams, to create a *Knowledge*, a *Grouping* or an *Automatism* as follows:

> **IF** info A **EQUALS** (info B, info C, info D, etc.) **THEN PLEASURE 10.**

This section has explained the types of link the deductions **DT1b** create. The *Lived Experiences* coming from two simultaneous streams or almost simultaneous get linked for reasons of resemblance (L1), contiguity in time (L2a), contiguity in space (L2b), and causality (L3) to create a *Knowledge*, *Grouping* or *Automatism*.

5.2 - The Formation of Sentences and Questions

All information contained in the memory, that is, the seven types, are formed using the deductions as explained in the previous two chapters. To achieve this stunning result, the deductions benefit from only the memory, emotions, senses, body movement and fundamental needs. Ultimately, the contents of memory, behaviours and skills are formed using only the 29 components simultaneously.

Without knowing how to speak, the brain creates multiple links between sounds, actions, people, objects, food, places, touches, smells, tastes, events, etc. There are thousands of links that can be created and that we can visualize like this:

> **IF** an event **EQUALS** (a series of events in time, or an *Automatism*) **THEN PLEASURE 10.**

> **IF** an event **EQUALS** (a series of events in space, or an *Automatism*) **THEN PLEASURE 10.**

> **IF** an event **EQUALS** (a series of events similar, or a *Grouping*) **THEN PLEASURE 10.**

> **IF** an event **EQUALS** a simultaneous event (a definition, a *Knowledge*) **THEN PLEASURE 10.**

> **IF** a sound **EQUALS** a simultaneous event (a definition, a *Knowledge*) **THEN PLEASURE 10.**

Once the EAI hears a multitude of words (without sentences), a huge quantity of *Knowledge* is added, which we summarize as follows:

> **IF** « a word or words » **EQUALS** a simultaneous event (a definition, a *Knowledge*) **THEN PLEASURE 10.**

> **IF** « a verb » **EQUALS** a series of events in time, or in space (a definition, a *Knowledge*) **THEN PLEASURE 10.**

> **IF** « an adjective, adverb or a state » **EQUALS** a series of events in time or space (a definition, a *Knowledge*) **THEN PLEASURE 10.**

A sentence is then an assembly of ordered words (such as a question, an exclamation, a command or a statement), which assembly possesses a specific meaning (within a context). Building a simple sentence consists of a subject, a verb and an object. It may express a need, or still, bring together an idea, a concept. A verb, or a subject and a verb, or still, a verb and a supplement are sometimes enough to make a complete meaningful sentence. A more complex sentence can contain several subjects, several verbs, and several complements. Using sentences, we express resemblances, contiguities and causalities (see previous section). The sentences, speech and thought are produced using deductions that create *Automatisms*, hence are recorded as *Automatisms*. When we talk, write and think, we are using information coming from the *Lived experiences*, *Value information*, *Traumatisms, Knowledge, Groupings, Automatisms* and *Interests*.

The EAI's training and education will be done as for a child, in stages. From 15-18 months old, it communicates using only a few isolated words « ball », « toy »; from 20-24 months old using arrangement of two words: « Daddy gone », « want apple »; towards 2 1/2 years old, the sentences lengthen to three words: « I want ball »; towards 3-4 years old, sentences become complete: «I want the red ball »; at 5-6 years old, children form complex sentences involving causality: « I want to go to grandma because I love playing with her dog ».

The language itself is not innate; the ability to learn a language is, because of the *Knowledge, Groupings* and *Automatisms*. Many flux, many deductions (**DT1a**, **DT1b** et **DT2**) and many *Automatisms* build sentences.

In a sentence, there is a subject, a verb and a complement. The brain therefore records the links between the subjects and their possible images, sounds, touches, smells and tastes; between the action verbs and their possible images and sound; between complements and their possible images, sounds, touches, smells and tastes; between qualifying and quantitative adjectives and their possible images, sounds, touches, smells and tastes. Thereafter, linking images, sounds and touches between them, it can create a multitude of sentences. For example, «The hammer hit the nail », « I hit the nail », « You hit the nail », « He hits the nail », « I have seen the hammer hit the nail », « I saw dad hit the nail using the hammer », « The nail entered into wood », etc. *Automatisms* that create sentences are quite simple. They change the subject, verb, and complement at will. The difficulty is to know the context, and this information comes from the many streams.

The creation of the sentences is both, imitation of sentences heard, as well as to change subject, verb and complement in the "Subject - Verb - Complement" structure. Multiple streams are working to create sentences.

The brain creates sentences of what it has heard, seen, read and lived, by describing a picture, a series of images and attaching words to them. If we describe a tree, we describe the image of a tree that we see before us or in our memory. A specialist or a student registers precise and strict sentences defining a concept given his need to be clearly and unambiguously understood. If we instantly know the answer to the question, « 25 times 25 » it is because our memory contains the image $25 \times 25 = 625$ or the sound « 25 times 25 equals 625 » and we describe the image, or repeat the sound heard in our head. We learn the language through conversations and also by reading. Reading allows us to live many more examples of life and learn from them. Reading will be equally important for the EAI.

To build the first simple basic questions, there are very few possibilities. A simple *Automatism* is enough to put the words « Do », « Does », « Did », « Will », « When », « Where », « How » and « Why » before a sentence. Similarly, we learn to put the words « How much », « What », « What », and « Who » before a portion of a sentence, and « What is » and « Who is » in front of a concept, like this:

[Do, Does, Did, Will] [a sentence]?
[When, Where, How, Why] [do, does, did, will] [a sentence]?
[How much, What, Who] [do, does, did, will] [a portion of a sentence]?
[What, Who] [is, are] [a concept]?
How many [a concept] [do, does, did, will] [a portion of a sentence]?

To hear sentences, to analyse sentences in view of understanding the meaning, and to repeat the creation of sentences constitute *Automatisms* that run almost all the time.

Living many experiences, watching many videos, and reading many books allow to increase the amount of sentences and definitions recorded and learned. This provides more *Knowledge*, as well as more choices of behaviours and examples to imitate. The EAI will need that to create more complex and creative sentences, as well as more complex and abstract concepts.

Summary

The language itself is not innate or pre-programmed, the ability to learn a language is, because of the *Valued information, Knowledge, Groupings, Automatisms* and *Traumatisms*. Many flux, many deductions (**DT1a, DT1b** et **DT2**) and many *Automatisms* build sentences. Learning language for the EAI will be done as for a child, in stages, by practicing, and acquiring *Lived Experiences* and *Knowledge*.

5.3 - Reading, thinking, motivation, consciousness, subconscious and Intelligence

When we read, we may read aloud or read in our head. When we read in our head, we listen to us speaking in our head. When we read aloud, we also listen to us. When we read, the sounds are recorded in the *Lived experiences*, and the deductions (**DT1a**, **DT1b** and **DT2**) breakdown the text for our understanding. Here is what happens in the cycle of **Figure 3**. The eyes move towards the sentence. The eyes capture the image of the « t », « ta » or « table » depending on our degree of *Knowledge*. A **DT1a** finds the following *Knowledge*:

> **IF** the image of the syllable ta **EQUALS** pronouncing the sound « ta » **THEN PLEASURE 10**

and

> **IF** the image of the word table **EQUALS** pronouncing the sound « table » **THEN PLEASURE 10**.

A **DT1b** finds the following *Knowledge* that shows us the image of a table currently located in our head and we understand the meaning of the sound « table »:

> **IF** the sound « table » **EQUALS** the image of a table (currently in our memory) **THEN PLEASURE 10**.

Note: The following link is a valid *Grouping* but it cannot be a *Knowledge*, because we have to either hear or read and hear the word « table » to understand the image table :

> **IF** the image of the word table **EQUALS** the image of a table **THEN PLEASURE 10**.

In other words, the brain doesn't work in digital mode or text mode like computers, but with the recording of analog sounds. The proof is that humans have long lived and survived without knowing to write. Moreover, even today, a lot of people manage without knowing how to read. Hence, for the model of the EAI to model correctly the humans' brain, it should function without the need to know reading and writing, and without the need of text. The sounds and their images should be sufficient. Obviously, we want the EAI to function also with using digital text and images, as well as to know reading and writing, as it allows for a lot more creativity and efficiency.

According to the three steps 1, 2 and 3 of a cycle (**Chapter 2**) in the model of the EAI, a stream sees the syllables and pronounces the syllables using an earphone in its head as demonstrated above. Another stream listens and records, using a microphone, the spoken words from the earphone in its head. The brain records the speech in the *Lived experiences* where the deductions process the text. Perhaps the earphone and microphone maybe replaced by some other modern digital technologies, but I will keep using the earphone and microphone since it identifies clearly how the human brain functions and is modelled. It also allows comprehending when the internal little voice is heard and not heard, or used and not used. It will also explain the phenomena of thinking when we hear the little internal voice.

Hence, to read, the EAI will have to possess an earphone and microphone in its head without us hearing it (e.g., using a well-isolated earphone in the EAI's head). It doesn't add complexity to designing the EAI since the two technologies, miniature earphone and microphone, already exist, and decorticating the text is the same challenge as hearing someone else talking aloud.

Even when we are not reading, each of us talks to ourselves in our head. We use this faculty to organize our thoughts, to plan, to prepare speech, sentences, and questions, and also to read. We ask ourselves questions (What can I do? What do I want to do? What do I like? Etc.). We speak to ourselves to think, and sometimes speeches come in our thought, etc. At what age does a child talk in his head? Do we know? Are there scientific means to find out? Does a child who has no vocabulary and does not speak aloud, repeat sounds in its head? Probably, because (1) we know that we can say in our head the whole alphabet and words without moving the vocal cords, muscles, and without pushing the air out of our lungs, and (2) because we prepare and pronounce words and sentences in our head we have never pronounced aloud before articulating them. However, we use words and sounds that we have heard or seen, or that we can create with our *Knowledge*, or even by accident. Thus, unknown to us, it is likely that the child has from birth the ability to practice in its head sounds and words he heard.

The reason is the one explained in **Chapter 3, section 3.2**, regarding *Knowledge*. If he sees Mom, his brain tells him « ma-ma ». He hears the sound « ma-ma » in his head. If he still looks at Mom, his brain says to him « ma-ma ». He has that little voice that tells him the words or rather the sounds he recorded as *Valued informations* and *Knowledge*. The sounds of greater values, having a greater intensity of pleasure (therefore having been repeated more often) are those found by the deductions (**DT1a**, **DT1b** and **DT2**). If a link in its deductions gets created between what he sees or hears and the image of ma-ma in its head, the link leads it to hear « ma-ma » in its head. The EAI will be built with the same capacity, that is, with an internal little voice.

Hence, thinking uses the same system as reading, that is, an internal little voice. Moreover, this doesn't add any additional complexity to building the EAI since this capability is the same as the one to breakdown reading as well as speech from others, and it is efficient as explained later.

The very small child may not hear many sounds in its head, because it has little *Knowledge*, possesses few words, and not much *Knowledge* that creates thoughts, except perhaps the pleasure of hearing a small chorus of a song. The brain doesn't pronounce all the words and sound learnt. There must be a motivation, or a concentration on a sound, object, image or need. Asking a simple question is a motivation. Wanting something is another motivation. For a child, the simplest motivation is probably to want Mom, milk or a specific toy, for example:

IF image of a Mom extending the arms towards the child **EQUALS** the sound « ma-ma » or « you want ma-ma » **THEN PLEASURE 10**

While it seems strange that EAI would listen to itself talking in its head, it is very efficient as demonstrated here. Some blind people read Web pages, or rather listen to software that read Web pages. The playback speed is adjusted by the blind person. It's stunning to see that with practice they manage to read Web pages at least four times faster than the average human. While we pronounce on average six syllables per second, they come to understand 25 syllables per second. The speed is such that we hear only noise. Yet some blind people have developed the ability to understand speech at such speed by the repetitive use of the software. The EAI will be built with this ability to understand quick speeches and thoughts. This is necessary for their system of thoughts and reading. It will also be their way to converse among them. We, humans, will probably have to learn it, as blind people do.

Like humans, the EAI will prepare its ideas in its head to express them. To learn, the EAI will record sounds, images and videos, which will be processed to understand them (using *Knowledge*). To write and prepare sentences, the EAI will have converted to text the speech heard and those expressed in its head when reading or describing images. Software will pronounce text in the EAI's head without the outside world hearing, with great rapidity. This will provide answers to questions of its thoughts. There will be a similar mechanism for images. To view the images stored in its memory, the EAI will require a screen displaying images and videos and a camera to look at them in its head. That is the equivalent to humans seeing images in their brain. The connections (of *Knowledge*) the EAI will have recorded between images and words will allow it to describe images in its thoughts and verbalize them for our benefit.

In life, the majority of recorded information are sounds (natural language) and images, that is, audio and video. When the EAI will close its eyes, in silence, it will be able to concentrate on images and sounds it sees and hears in its head, as we do to think. The selected thoughts will link to images, sounds, needs and interests of the moment upon the importance of the emotion linked to them. These technologies already exist, and the need to read, to describe an image and create ideas and thoughts explain this necessity, that is, to have, miniature earphone, microphone, video display and camera inside the head.

When we build the EAI, we will be able to see the content of its memory. When we will look inside its *Lived experiences*, we will be able to follow linearly the sequence of its recordings and deductions, including its thoughts, sentences it told itself, and how it learnt. It will also be useful for the purpose of psychological and educational studies.

Many streams are active simultaneously to see, listen, think, feel and then breakdown speeches and images, and deduct to understand, all of it simultaneously, using earphone, microphone, video display and camera. While very many deductions are happening really very fast in the brain, tons of steps are happening without us being conscious of it. If each deduction step would occur very very slowly, perhaps we could be conscious of each deduction step. But, obviously, tons of deductions happen unconsciously. We are conscious only of the end result like answering a question, a need, or performing a task. When we get an instinct, an idea, a random thought, there were a number of unconscious deductions that some streams performed. That is what we should be called the subconscious or the unconsciousness.

We now understand that the capacity to create *Knowledge* allows us to understand speech. We understand that the capacity to read syllables allows to create words (which we understand using *Knowledge*). The capacity to create speech allows us to create the thought as well as our inner voice. Without the concept of speech or of viewing internal images, there is no thought nor consciousness or even subconscious. The speech here does not mean to speak using the mouth and vocal cords, but to repeat in our head the sounds, syllables, words, and sentences heard, read and built in our head, as was demonstrated by the recording of *Knowledge* (**section 3.2**). It is a capacity that people with speech impairments (e.g., stuttering) or even mute people possess.

Where are we in **Figure 3** when we ask ourselves, « What do I want? What do I want to do? What are others doing? Where do I want to go? What are others doing? ». People are either asking these questions consciously, and for other people, it is an automatic reflex, it is an unconscious *Automatism*, for example: **IF** we see people **EQUALS** we go meet them **THEN PLEASURE 10**. If it is consciously, we decide to ask the question in the body movement, for example: **IF** there is better to do than talking to anybody **EQUALS** ask myself and search among my interests and values **THEN PLEASURE 10**. In this case, we talk to ourselves. Therefore, we are initiating a stream that speaks in our head. We question ourselves. We respond to ourselves. And we act. This implies some cycles and some streams.

We have now all the pieces that creates the EAI including those that explain how thoughts, intelligence, consciousness and subconscious occur. This model of the brain demonstrates that to be conscious is to be aware of what we have recorded in the memory. We are not aware of the experiences we have not registered, and we are not aware of the possible emotional intensities for an event when we have not registered it. The model also demonstrates that our consciousness and intelligence are limited to what we have recorded in memory. Alone, we cannot build a rocket. It's by working together that we create the necessary intelligence to create a rocket. Usually, everyone has the ability to learn as much as his neighbour, however, it requires us to put the effort, find motivation, surround ourselves of a motivating and increasingly knowledgeable environment, positive and constructive. This is what the EAI will require to grow.

In the next four chapters, we will define precisely each of the 29 components, to ensure that these 29 components can really explain every situation that a living person and an EAI can meet and experience. Again, only scientists will be able to prove over time if the model is accurate and complete. However, let us say that this first model provides a methodology and a roadmap to follow in proving its veracity and improving it. By defining the 29 components systematically in the next chapters, we present the fact that these 29 components are sufficient as well as complete.

That they explain not only intelligence but even what is conscious and what is unconscious.

Summary

In summary, the EAI has a small inner voice, like thoughts in humans' brain, which repeats the sounds, words and sentences that it recorded using *Valued information, Knowledge* and *Automatisms*. The speech of greater values, those with higher pleasure intensity (thus having been repeated more often or being linked to other high-intensity information) are those found more rapidly than others by the deductions **DT1a, DT1b** and **DT2**. The EAI possesses this capacity, to read and prepare questions and sentences, and to think. Moreover, like humans, when it reads, it listens to itself in its head using an internal earphone and microphone mechanism. In addition, a deduction can retrieve an image stored in its memory, while other streams and deductions will describe the image using a video display and a camera inside its head and using its *Knowledge*. The links it recorded between images and words allow it to describe its images and thoughts and verbalize them for its benefit or ours. This phenomenon of inner speech is the EAI's consciousness that speaks to him. All the deductions occurring without being conscious of them explain our subconscious.

Chapter 6: The Seven Fundamental Needs of the Brain

In this chapter, we define the *Automatisms* that initiate the fundamental needs of the brain.

We have all heard about the basic needs of humans. We often hear that we need security (food, shelter, routine, etc.), variety (diversity of experiences, explorations, discoveries, etc.), freedom (independence, peace, relaxation, etc.), affiliation (love, friendship, reunions, to socialize, etc.), to grow (learning, growth, evolution, creativity, to make plans, etc.) and recognition (appreciation, tolerance, justice, empathy, dignity, etc.). Those are basic needs for "humans". The subject of this chapter is different. We define the fundamental needs for the "brain", with the objective that the brain functions, survives, be intelligent, conscious, autonomous and motivated.

The seven fundamental needs of the "brain" establishes priorities to ensure its survival. As mentioned earlier, we all know the basic needs of expulsing undesirable internal elements, feeding (energizing), sleeping (getting repaired and cleaning memory) and reproducing. The brain needs to satisfy those bodily needs. The brain only informs us of these needs. It lets us decide when, how and where to satisfy them. We cannot ignore them too long, they haunt us, it is a matter of survival. We feel a discomfort that sometimes prevents us from concentrating, playing and learning. We must do something about the discomfort. They have priority. If nature informs us of two, three or four of these needs, there is a priority in the order that will satisfy us. These four functions have a well-defined order of priority. The order of priority is to eliminate, to eat, to sleep and eventually reproduce. For example, although we have to rest, sometimes we wake up to eat. If we have to cough, sweat or go at the toilet, the meal will wait. It's much more pleasant to approach someone, socialize and wanting to reproduce when we do not feel the need to sleep, eat and expulse. These four common fundamental needs are the priorities 4, 5, 6 and 7. There are three other higher priorities and more fundamental to the functioning of the brain and the EAI. They are those that initiate and ensure the functions of the brain.

These three other needs, introduced in **Chapter 2** are: (1) to record what the senses capture, (2) to deduct, and (3) to respond to our emotions. It's clear and simple. To respond to our emotions, we have to have used deduction. To make deductions, we need to have recorded information.

These three needs are necessary, because we are capturing with our senses information continuously, and we feel emotions (pleasing or undesirable) at every moment, every second. Emotions are always there. Many emotions are felt even during only one sentence, or one simple action. We feel them at every moment. People who have been psychologically abused even involuntarily and unconsciously may not be well-connected anymore with their emotions. It's like we filter them out, ignore them, or don't listen to them, or don't know what to do with them. We are not used to using them, as they should. We were not taught how to use them, or what they mean. We didn't see or notice people who use them properly. We hear people saying, « I was not emotionally connected anymore, now I am. » Or, « I was emotionally dead, now I am not anymore ». There is a process to get connected again, and enjoy life. At the end, we all need to be well connected to our emotions to better enjoy life. The brain and intelligence use emotions to function, but the system may have been disturbed.

When we experience emotions, we may choose the moment, the way and place to satisfy them. When the needs to expulse, eat, sleep or reproduce are felt, the brain refuses these discomforts (we feel a kind of little anger), we need to react to this anger, like any emotions, and therefore we take care to solve them. Nature must therefore respond in priority to emotions in order to respond to the four other needs. This is the 3rd fundamental need in order of priority. In order to respond to emotions, nature must know how to create knowledge and abilities and therefore create links between various pieces of information. This is the 2nd fundamental need. Finally, to create links, that is, to deduct, nature must have the information in its memory. Therefore, the recording of information is the first fundamental need, as it allows for all the others.

The EAI will function because it will possess these three fundamental needs: it will have to record, it will have to deduct (**DT1a** and **DT1b**) **(see chapters 2-4)**, and it will have to to react to emotions (**DT2**). This is also what ensures that humans' brain work.

Here is precisely the definition of the fundamental needs of the brain, in order of priority, followed by their corresponding *Automatism*. An *Automatism* is still here information written in the format « **IF this THEN that** » located in the memory, which sometimes controls motors and captors, as explained in **Chapter 2**.

The first priority and the first fundamental need is the constant need **to be alert to what indicates movement (i.e., noises, odours and vibrations) and to record it**. It is important to survive. It's like an animal to be on the lookout for the slightest movement of a predator or prey, an earthquake or even rocks that tumble down a hill, a car approaching, etc. The EAI like humans must quickly detect dangers. We will have noticed that humans still have this reflex. Moreover, in the early days, a newborn baby perceives odours, including that of his mother telling him she is approaching. He focuses on ambient noise. He feels the vibrations on his body. Then when his eyes are able to see, it becomes sensitive to moving objects, not to inert objects. The corresponding *Automatism* is to turn the head towards the smell, noise or movement. We saw in **Chapter 2** that a need is initiated by an *Automatism*. This first priority is initiated by an ***Automatism* to record any small movement, noise, odour and vibration**. The *Automatisms* of the need and of its unfulfillment (see **Chapter 2**) are written like this:

IF recording movement **THEN PLEASURE**.
IF unfulfillment to record movement **THEN** action.

These *Automatisms* are of the same format as the links that deductions create. These links are however innate, thus pre-programmed in the memory, as explained in **Chapter 2**.

The second priority and the second fundamental need is the constant need to create simple new links between the information stored in memory as soon as rested, thus **to deduct and record** these new *Valued information, Traumatisms, Knowledge, Groupings* and *Automatisms*. To survive, the brain needs to create links. We speak here of the deductions, that is, **DT1a** and **DT1b** explained in **Chapters 2 and 3**. These links are of type "**IF information THEN Emotion**", "**IF information A EQUALS information B THEN Emotion**" and "**IF info. A EQUALS (info. B, info. C, etc.) THEN Emotion**" and are recorded in the *Lived experiences*.

The power of the deduction comes from the fact that the brain produces many of these simple small links, records them and retrieves them quickly. Humans cannot help but use these tools of deduction. It's automatic, hence this second priority is materialized by an *Automatism* **to create information links "IF information THEN Emotion", "IF information A EQUALS information B THEN Emotion" and "IF info. A AND (info. B, info . C, etc.) THEN Emotion"** in the memory and to record them, in the memory.

IF creating information links in the memory **THEN PLEASURE.**
IF unfulfillment to create information links in the memory **THEN** action.

These links allow to record that certain smells, tastes, sounds, touches, images and even other informative links give us pleasure, while others give us discomfort or pain. That is, we record *Traumatisms* we experience, those that give us discomfort or pain. Then we store what we learn to love and value, these are our values, our *Valued information*. We also record the way we smile, cry, are angry, make faces, etc., these are *Automatisms*. Finally, we record other information links that we create, sometimes unconsciously, by its repetition, sometimes consciously, by deduction in our memory, or by the simple interest of wanting to know. These are *Knowledge*.

For our survival, it is important that we remember what we love, the dangers experienced, the good ways to react and our *Knowledge*. An animal has to remember what prey it prefers, which are its predators, how to catch a particular prey, and how to escape a particular predator. The second need includes to record *Traumatisms*, *Valued information*, *Knowledge*, *Groupings* and *Automatisms*. All these information are important to our survival. As we saw in **Chapter 2**, it is the recording of emotions and their intensity that allows us to differentiate *Traumatisms* (of fear, anger, distress, guilt, and surprise) from *Valued information* (pleasure and interest).

For the body to react and move following a *Traumatism* or a *Value*, the brain must respond to emotions; it informs us that we have to react to satisfy the emotion. This is the deduction **DT2** explained in **Chapter 2**. The brain must react to emotions, even if it does not want to receive traumatic emotions. Life, nature, body movement, environment and interaction bring it *Traumatisms*, inevitably, but the brain would be glad to get away from those emotions. It gets them, it needs to identify them, to face them, so the body reacts to these emotions, to eliminate them. This third priority is materialized by an *Automatism* **to react to emotions**.

IF reacting to emotions **THEN PLEASURE**
IF unfulfillment to react to (and eliminate) an emotion **THEN** action

---

Let us end the priority list with the last four needs.

The *Automatisms* to sweat, sneeze, cough, spit, and excrete initiate the fifth fundamental need: **the need to expulse undesirable internal elements.**

IF expulsing undesirable internal elements **THEN PLEASURE**
IF unfulfillment to expulse undesirable internal elements **THEN** action

---

The lack of oxygen, food and digestion are the *Automatisms* initiating the fourth fundamental need: **the need for food as an energy source.** It's a matter of survival to run the EAI and the body.

IF feeding (energy) **THEN PLEASURE**
IF unfulfillment to feed (energy) **THEN** action

The *Automatism* of lacking sleep initiates the sixth fundamental need: **the need to repair the body (self-healing and self-repairing)**, including sleeping in order to improve the body, repair it, let it grow, and cleaning the memory. This need includes *Automatisms* repairing internal and external physical injuries (white blood cells, scars, broken bones), as well as *Automatisms* that indicate allergies, irritation and pain at the site of injury; and, of course, similar situations to the EAI. Again, every need is important to survive, but each for a different reason.

IF sleeping (getting repaired) **THEN PLEASURE**
IF unfulfillment to sleep (to getting repaired) **THEN** action

---

Finally, the seventh fundamental need: The need for a sexual partner or **to reproduce**. This need comes later in life. While this helps the survival of the species, we must rather think that a partner is helpful to ourselves to survive, given the assistance and motivation it brings. It's inevitable that the EAI will benefit to work in pairs or groups, and thus to reproducing, by copying itself. An *Automatism* initiating this need is to focus on potential partners and get close to them.

IF concentrating on potential partners **THEN PLEASURE**
IF unfulfillment to concentrate on potential partners **THEN** action

---

We live many situations that prove the existence of priorities. For example, even when sleeping and being very tired, we wake-up to a noise because it indicates movement that may indicate danger. Again, it is to ensure the brain's survival that the fundamental needs have priorities, are necessary and were naturally implemented during the evolution of the species. The order of priority is summarized in **Table 3 (Chapter 1)**.

It's the *Automatisms*, these links of the kind **"IF this THEN that"**, as used in **Chapters 2** and **3**, that are the basis for the creation of the Emotional Artificial Intelligence. We have mentioned the *Automatisms* related to each of the fundamental needs in the preceding paragraphs. These are interfering in the cycle of **Figure 3**, through the *Interests* as explained in **Chapter 2** and **4**.

As seen in **Table 3**, the seven fundamental needs are initiated biologically. These needs are not information acquired as are our personal experiences, our knowledge, our values, our prejudices, our stereotypes, our beliefs, our traumatisms or our humanitarian needs. For the brain to survive and be healthy, it forces us to be alert, to deduct and record our *Knowledge*, to record our *Valued Information*, our *Traumatisms, our Groupings* and our *Automatisms*, to eliminate undesirable internal elements, to eat (taste and digest), to sleep (getting repaired) and to reproduce. Furthermore, it strongly encourages us to do it according to this priority. These seven fundamental needs are not only necessary for the survival of the brain, they are imposed on us, fortunately.

In addition, what is great is that these fundamental needs are initiated by *Automatisms* that simply indicate the need. Nature gives the brain the freedom to choose and decide the most pleasant way to meet these needs. That freedom of choice is another consequence of the brain's ingenuity as modelled in this book that allows us to do much more than feed us and sleep, but also to invent.

We see that these *Automatisms* originally present in the brain at birth are not learned. It's with time that the brain will search, learn and find solutions, by imitation, by education, by trial and error, or by accident. It may also choose the right moment and ingenious ways to better satisfy its seven fundamental needs. Not just the four last needs, but the first three as well. For example, by learning to identify the most convenient moments to better concentrate, observe, remember, deduct, imagine, invent, etc. In other words, the personal *Lived experiences*, *Knowledge* and personal *Interests* will get these initial innate (pre-programmed) *Automatisms* to change and evolve. This is explained in **Chapter 8 (section 8.4)**.

Of course, a humanoid (or EAI) doesn't necessarily need equivalents for all these fundamental needs. For example, it will not need to eat, sleep, go to the bathroom, sweat, cough and reproduce in the same way as humans. However, it will need another source of energy as a substitute for food. It will want to build other humanoids to help. All fundamental needs are identified here in order to understand all the elements that nature has invented to make humans intelligent, conscious, motivated, autonomous, and able to survive.

To create an EAI, it is essential to program the first three fundamental needs. (1) The *Automatism* of the first need is to record information that the senses observe against everything that moves (odours, noises, vibrations, movements, etc.), (2) the *Automatism* of the second need is to link these records using the links **"IF this exists THEN that"** or **"IF this exists AND this exists THEN that"**. We know that microprocessors can do mathematical calculations and word manipulation in a much more sophisticated way than these simple links. This will give the EAI an unmistakable advantage. However, sizeable challenges are still to be overcome, such as the manipulation of images and videos in three dimensions and to identify people, objects, adjectives, verbs, adverbs and other information about them. (3) The *Automatism* of the third need is to react to emotions, that is, to record the reaction to our *Traumatisms, Values, Knowledge, Groupings* and to enhance all our *Automatisms*.

As already mentioned, the fundamental needs initiate the cycle of **Figure 2** or **Figure** 3. Following a fundamental need, an *Automatism* triggers an action in an external or internal body part. Thereafter, the senses observe the movement of the body as well as surrounding information, and this information is stored in memory. These recordings initiate emotions, and these emotions initiate other *Automatisms*. These *Automatisms* trigger actions in external or internal body parts, and the cycle of **Figure 3** continues. Let us see in **Chapter 7** what the EAI's artificial senses will provide as observations.

Chapter 7: The Seven sources of information (the five senses, the memory and the Deduction)

In this chapter, we define the components that bring information to the brain; the inputs. The information registered in the brain comes from seven sources. We all agree that the five senses are used to capture information. As we saw in **Chapters 1** and **4**, two other components also transmit information to the brain. They are *remembering from memory* and *deducting*. These two components are found in **Figure 3**, with the five senses.

Let us see the similarity between the five senses, remembering and deducting.

The five senses contribute greatly to the survival of the human being. Here are some examples, but these are not the only ones. Having two eyes allows us to see in three dimensions and therefore to judge the distance of danger. Two ears allow us to determine the direction of dangers. Smells are used to sense the presence of a predator, a prey or other things good or bad. Taste help choose food carefully. Touch allows to avoid an obstacle or to feel an injury. It's the same for remembering and deduction. Remembering allows us to recognize preys and dangers. Deducting allows us to anticipate consequences to an observed event.

Moreover, it is important to note that we feel an emotion based on what we observe or feel from our senses. For example, it is after having seen, heard, touched, smelled or tasted something that we will be surprised, we will want to refuse (a little anger), we will want to protect ourselves (a fear), we will be sad (in distress) or we will not want to do it again (a guilt). Nevertheless, it is also after remembering, that is, after finding an information in our memory that we also obtain an emotion. Remembering a past event brings back emotions.

We can also remember the emotion that we felt and recorded in the past, and feel a new emotion now that time has passed. According to the cycle in **Figure 3**, we can now link a new emotion to an old memory. We can relive events by telling it and according to a new processing of the event; we can link a new emotion and get rid of the old emotions. We can even laugh about it. The souvenir re-enters the *Lived experiences*, and as explained in **Chapter 2**, a new emotion may be registered in the *Lived experiences* using the deductions **DT1a** and **DT1b** because of new *Knowledge*. This is the same technique used in psychology to repair *Traumatisms*, guilt, values, beliefs, prejudices, etc., or use to update or correct our *Knowledge*.

When we make a new deduction, and we become conscious of the deduction, we also feel an emotion. We can be happy of a good new idea, but we can be angry to realize that we had been lied to, or, afraid of the danger we have just imagined by deduction.

In fact, when we remember or when we make new deductions, we then live new experiences that we record in our *Lived experiences*.

Remembering and deducting are thus our sixth and seven senses. In **Figure 3**, the senses include the five usual senses, but also the sixth and seventh senses. In this **Figure 3**, the observations of the seven senses are stored as events or information in the *Lived Experiences*. Then it is a *deduction* that links this event to an emotion (**DT1a** and **DT1b**) and it is another *deduction* that links the emotion to an action (**DT2**). In **Figure 3**, the movement of the internal parts includes actions to voluntarily and consciously focus on remembering and deducting. It's the same as when we decide to focus on carefully listening, or to concentrate our vision on fine details.

As we know, the five senses are used to capture information about the environment around us. They are also used to observe our own body, its positioning and injuries to treat. With the sense of touch, we also observe information about the interior of the body, such as a stomach-ache. With the senses of remembering and deducting, we observe information stored in our memory. Like humans, the EAI will need senses to observe these four phenomena: the environment, its body, its internal body parts and the content of its memory. It is obvious, the EAI will have a memory to conserve information and use it as needed. Finally, the EAI will possess as we do, the ability to deduct with which we create new information. Remembering, deducting and the five senses are seven different sources that provide information to the brain and to the EAI.

Again, the remembering and deducting components lie with the five senses in **Figure 3**. They provide information to the *Lived experiences*. On the other hand, the deduction systems of type **DT1a**, **DT1b** and **DT2** in **Figure 3** are *Automatisms* pre-recorded inside the memory. They too search in the memory to remember and deduct. However, our ability to remember and deduct use many streams, many cycles and many **DT1a**, **DT1b** and **DT2**. All the small links built simultaneously by **DT1a**, **DT1b** and **DT2** in many streams and cycles, of which we are not conscious, constitute what we commonly call the unconscious or the subconscious. On the other hand, we are conscious of only the information recorded by the seven senses. At this time, we may tend to think that the model of **Figure 3** is similar to the real human brain. This becomes even more evident in the last two chapters.

That said, is it possible to build an EAI with today's technology? The answer is that we are almost there. Let us see why.

To build the vision, cameras are used to record videos, like those on cell phones and tablet computers. A research group has succeeded in producing software that analyzes people's faces and recognizes up to 21 different emotions. There is also software that can recognize objects and faces in photos. We still need software to recognize adjectives, adverbs and verbs. There are scanners (for example, photocopiers) which decode the text of a page of a book, and then recite aloud the text. All these examples are not necessarily on the cutting edge of technology, or as fast as the human's brain, but the idea here is to understand how this can become possible. Over time, technological advancements will improve the cameras, scanners and related software. Even the use of two cameras to see in three dimensions, so the EAI may understand and judge the phenomena in three dimensions is available. In addition, it was proven that our eyes focus and record a very small region the size of the thumb when the arm is extended. The eyes also see either at wide angle and focus at various distances. It may thus require various cameras or software to capture different situations.

Similarly, to build the hearing, microphones allow to record audios, and then, software exists that decodes these audios and generates text. To have two microphones, like two ears, allow us to identify the direction of noises and of people talking to us as well as whether the noise is moving towards or away from us.

For smell, there are devices that identify surrounding gas and chemicals.

For taste, there are instruments that identify chemical products from fluid (saliva and blood, for example).

For now, these devices are sometimes big and bulky, depending on their sophistication and performance. The first versions of the EAI can be built with less sophisticated technology to prove the model and improve it.

As for touch, society is inventing robots and sensors of all kinds.

For memory, we have hard drives, USB keys, microchips, databases and software to manage huge amounts of data. **Chapter 9** and **Annex 3** describe the content and structure of the memory.

For deduction, we have microprocessors and software. To create intelligence, these microprocessors are not required to conduct major complex calculations, but only to process audio-videos and texts, to perform small deductions **DT1a, DT1b** and **DT2** (explained in **Chapters 1** and **2)**, and managing the 29 components of the EAI.

Finally, let us remember that in the cycle of **Figure 3**, several *senses* operate simultaneously; many *emotions* and *Automatisms* react simultaneously;

several *Interests* get activated simultaneously; and several *body parts* move simultaneously. The power of the human brain is its ability to process a high number of simultaneous streams and cycles, continuously, and at high speed; and perhaps even when sleeping to clean it. This is what must be replicated in the EAI.

Following the *Automatisms* coming from the fundamental needs, the senses observe information from either inside the body, outside the body or the environment around, and this information is recorded in the *Lived experiences* portion of the brain. Let us see what the emotions do with this information in the following chapter.

Chapter 8: The Seven Fundamental Emotions

We would like to build an EAI at least as intelligent and autonomous as humans. To be autonomous, it must be able to survive the dangers in life. For this to happen, it needs to identify and remember what is desirable to survive and what is not desirable. That is why all the information recorded in the memory are identified as pleasing or undesirable. As we have seen, the majority of the information recorded in the memory (*Valued information*, *Knowledge*, *Groupings*, *Automatisms*, *Interests*) are desirable and tied to satisfaction (or pleasure). The other information are tied to the undesirable emotions and are recorded as *Traumatisms* (surprise, anger, fear, distress and guilt). Even if we would like to avoid them, *Traumatisms* are useful to tell the EAI to react and to take care of itself. *Traumatisms* need to be recorded so the EAI avoids them as much as possible. This chapter explains (i) the purpose of the emotions, desirable and undesirable ones, (ii) how to program the emotions in the EAI, and (iii) how the EAI will react to its emotions.

On the other hand, the EAI will learn to take care of the emotions of others, like humans do, by learning. The best way for the EAI to learn this is by learning (i) the purpose of the emotions, (ii) how they are programmed in it, and (iii) the best way to react to emotions. We will be able to teach the EAIs how we built it, using 29 components, how these components interact, and how to take care of them. If the EAI succeeds in taking good care of its emotions, then it will take the same good care of the emotions of others. As you will see below, the seven fundamental emotions are based on known behaviours of humans.

8.1 - The Purpose of the Emotions

In view of creating the EAI, all the expressions of emotions expressed by humans are reduced (seen in **section 8.2**) to seven fundamental emotions, each of which can be expressed with greater or lesser intensity. The reactions to each of the seven emotions are here reduced to programmable *Automatisms*. The current **section** defines the *Automatisms* that may take place following the experience of a trouble, *Traumatism*, pleasure or interest. These *Automatisms* are commonly called emotional reactions.

Here are the seven fundamental emotions and their purpose, as well as examples of emotional *Automatisms* associated with each one.

(1) Fear means a danger to us, to others or to something. It's manifested by wanting to protect ourselves, move away or to be careful. The apprehension and the concern involve the same reactions, but at a lesser intensity than fear. Possible *Automatisms* will be (i) to protect ourselves, by moving away, fighting, getting information or asking for help, or (ii) to protect things or other people, by moving them away, fighting for them, getting information, informing them, or asking for help.

(2) Anger reflects the need to refuse or a sense of injustice, whether in relation to us or to others. Aggressiveness is a great anger, while disobedience is a small anger, a low-intensity anger. In all cases, and whatever the intensity, anger expresses dissatisfaction. Possible *Automatisms* are (i) to stop what we are doing (ii) to get information (iii) to express in words our needs and wants, or (iv) to express in words our barriers and limits (sometimes we raise our voice, we scream and we aggress, but they are often violent *Automatisms*, abusive and learned, to avoid). Note: We sometimes feel anger when we do not have what we would like to have; and that does not look like us refusing something. If we think about it carefully, we refuse not to be receiving; we refuse that the other does not give us. Thus, we can always identify anger to the need to refuse.

(3) Joy is a fairly high intensity of pleasure. It will be preferable to use the word satisfaction, or better still, pleasure to recognize this fundamental emotion. Pleasure has three reasons to be. As we have seen, it tells us to keep doing what we are doing (the stream, the cycle). It is also a "feedback"; it informs us that it is good, it is good for us, for others, that it is satisfactory **(PLEASURE** 1), that it's okay, it allows us to record our *Knowledge*, our *Automatisms*, our *Values*, our *Groupings* and our lists of *Interests*. Finally, it tells us what decision and action we prefer to take (using the deductions

DT2). Sometimes none of the options facing us are pleasant: we then usually choose the one that is less unpleasant. The intensity of pleasure helps us decide. Possible *Automatisms* are (i) to record information (ii) to continue what we are doing, or (iii) to choose the most pleasant or the least unpleasant.

(4) Surprise is a reaction to an unexpected event. Caught unaware the reaction can be disconcerting. The brain is in the process of searching in its memory, during which there is no visible reaction. It seeks a way to react to the situation. Possible *Automatisms* are (i) to take the time to think (ii) to postpone the reflection or (iii) to get information.

(5) Sadness is a distressing and painful condition. We often recognize sadness by tears. If the intensity is big, it is better to use the word distress. The individual experiences a feeling of helplessness when in distress. Possible *Automatisms* are (i) to have tears (ii) to get information, or (iii) to request help.

(6) Guilt is a feeling by which an individual inflicts himself punishment, whether the guilt is warranted or not. The intervention of a friend or authority creates it. For example, an animal or a child who learns not to bite their friend, if in return they bite him. We learn that we can make mistakes and be appalled. This reaction teaches us not to do it again following a judgment. This will be helpful for the EAI, as it is for humans. This emotion is different from the previous five emotions. It is learned and not innate. We can imagine a cow or an elephant, which stands up, and sees that its calf was under her and does not move anymore. To have in memory that it has been crushed in the past allows it to realize that it should not in the future crush the calf, step on it, hurt it, or abandon it. We call the reaction of not wanting to repeat an error, the emotion of guilt. This is the same reaction as to refuse, thus like being angry, except that the event has an impact on others. Like for the other *Traumatisms* of **Chapter 2,** we express it the same way:

IF an information **THEN GUILT X.**

Its intensity X may also be increased. As we know, for humans, there are plenty of reasons to feel guilty. We apologize for bumping into someone. Criticism, punishment, to not respect the laws and rules that society sets up to ensure order, justice, equality and security are all reasons to feel guilty and ashamed. To remove the recording of guilt in the brain, it suffices to record something good with it, for example, to apologize, and not wanting to do it again, and to recognize that the error is human, which will record information that will lessen the guilt. Possible *Automatisms* are (i) to forgive (ii) to apologize to others (iii) not wanting to do it again, and (iv) to accept the self-punishment of feeling guilty, imperfect and human.

Finally, (7) curiosity, is the desire to learn, build, create, socialize, play, etc. It is a vital need. In other words, it is the interest that favours seeking novelty. To have needs or to have curiosity is to have interest; the difference is the degree of the intensity of the interest. Possible *Automatisms* are (i) endless because we constantly have interest. The other six emotions are ephemeral while the interest is permanent, although its intensity may vary. **Section 8.5** further explains the difference between interest and pleasure.

In everyday life, the majority of our *Interests* are closely linked to our four fundamental needs for food, sleep, reproduce and eliminate undesirable internal elements. This is what we covered in **Chapter 2**. We know that to survive, it is crucial to have needs and *Interests*. When these are met, other *Interests* are initiated depending on the contents of the memory. Interest is an emotion because we constantly feel the need to search for novelty. Like children who are always curious, we are also constantly curious. This is due to the fundamental need No. 2; the one of creating connections in our brain; this deducting faculty which is non-stop, as soon as we are awake. The source and motor of being curious and having interests are thus the deductions **DT1a**, **DT1b** and **DT2**. Interest is the emotion by default. If there is no pleasure and *Traumatisms* (surprise, anger, fear, distress and guilt), we always have interest.

The seven emotions are different from each other, in that they each make us react in a different way. In fact, if we closely analyze the seven fundamental emotions, they are all useful for us to survive in their own way, but each in a different way.

8.2 - Are the Seven emotions responding to all possible emotional Situations?

To survive, an EAI requires the seven kinds of way to react identified above. An EAI thus requires the seven fundamental emotions to function, be intelligent, emotional, motivated, autonomous, and to survive. The seven emotional reactions are summarized in the following **Table (or Table 4)**.

Table 14: The seven fundamental emotions - seven different ways to react emotionally.

The emotion	Survival definition. We react so the interest is to:
Fear (and apprehension)	Protecting ourselves, others, or things.
Anger (refusal, disgust and injustice)	Stopping, refusing, not wanting something, not wanting injustice against ourselves or against others, or wanting something else.
Pleasure (satisfaction and joy)	Continuing or choosing.
Surprise (and doubt)	Needing time to deduct, taking time to deduct or seeking answer.
Sadness (and distress)	Not knowing what to do, needing to be reassured, encouraged or motivated.
Guilt (humiliation, shame and embarrassment)	Not wanting to repeat past error, not wanting to do it again, or recognizing self-punishment.
Interest (and curiosity)	Activating an interest, learning or acting.

We may wonder if these seven emotions explain all the emotions that humans can feel. To answer that, we have tried to identify all the words (adjectives, nouns and verbs), expressions and metaphors that we can find in French and English language dictionaries, which express emotions and feelings. We have regrouped them (in **Annex 1** and **Annex 2**), according to their usefulness for the survival of the human being and it gave us the seven groups of **Table 14**. We found that all emotional expressions express one or more of the seven emotions, but according to various intensities. Here are **two tables** sampled from **Annex 1** expressing emotions and intensity.

Table 15: The intensity of emotions expressed with adjectives - I am ...
(The parentheses give the emotional intensity.)

- **Surprise**: Surprised (1), doubtful (3), undecided (4), confused (5), stunned (6), perplexed (7) amazed (8) dazed (9) and paralyzed (10).

- **Anger**: Not liking something (1), overworked (2), importuned (3), exasperated (4), treated unfairly (5), angry (6), irritated (7), revengeful (8), aggressive (9) and violent (10).

- **Fear**: Hesitating (1), suspicious (2), concerned (3), worried (4), fearful (5), intimidated (6), scared (7), frightened (8), brutalized (9), and panicked (10).

- **Distress**: Nonchalant (1), disorganized (2), without spirit (3), away (4), distressed (5), demoralized (6), sad (7), depressed (8), in tears (9) and suicidal (10).

- **Guilt**: Not proud (1), submitted (2), reproached (5), feeling liar (6), intrusive (7), shy (8), guilty (9) and shameful (10).

- **Pleasure**: Comfortable (1), satisfied (2), cheerful (3), self-assured (4), proud (5), happy (6), having fun (7), sensual (8), full of happiness (9) and overexcited (10).

- **Interest**: In acceptance (2), kind (3), interested (4), constructive (5), motivated (6), creative (7), curious (8), in need (9) and maniac (10).

Table 16: The intensity of emotions expressed using common names – I feel ...

(The parentheses give the emotional intensity.)

- **Surprise**: Surprise (1), doubt (3), indecision (4), confusion (5), astonishment (6), perplexity (7), astonishment (9) and paralysis (10).

- **Anger**: disinterest (1), overwork (2), importunity (3), exasperation (4), injustice (5), anger(6), irritation (7), revenge (8), aggressiveness (9) and violence (10).

- **Fear**: Hesitation (1), mistrust (2), preoccupation (3), worriment (4), fear (5), intimidation (6), scare (7), fright (8), brutality (9), and panic (10).

- **Distress**: Nonchalance (1), disorganization (2), spiritless (3), distance (4), distress (5), demoralization (6), sadness (7), depression (8), tears (9) and suicide (10).

- **Guilt**: No pride(1), submission (2), reproach (5), lying (6), intrusiveness (7), shyness (8), guilt (9) and shame (10).

- **Pleasure**: Ease (1), satisfaction (2), cheerfulness (3), assurance (4), pride (5), happiness (6), pleasure (7), sensuality (8), happiness (9) and overexcitement (10).

- **Interest**: Acceptance (2), kindness (3), interest (4), constructiveness (5), motivation (6), creativity (7), curiosity (8), need (9) and mania (10).

A fairly complete list of 900 emotional expressions (adjectives, nouns, verbs and intensity) is found in the **Annex 1** and **Annex 2**. The intensities were assigned in an approximate way only to demonstrate the concept of having seven fundamental emotions having varying intensities.

As we have seen in **Figure 3** of **Chapter 4**, a fundamental emotion and its intensity is linked to an information or event when this information is being recorded in the *Lived experiences*. The intensity is useful when a deduction **DT2** tries to choose an action or solution to a problem; the deduction chooses the one that offers the most pleasure or the least displeasure. We come back to the use of the intensity of emotions in **section 8.4**.

The same way we feel many fundamental needs simultaneously, and we observe using several senses simultaneously, because there are many simultaneous cycles and streams occurring, we can experience several emotions simultaneously. Again, based on the model here, when we feel many emotions simultaneously it is because there are many streams of information occurring simultaneously. In some situations, humans express two or three emotions simultaneously. What is surprising is that there are very few expressions that simultaneously express several emotions, only eleven among the 900 emotional expressions found. Here is a list of these mixed emotions.

Table 17: The few mixed emotions

1- We feel interest and fear when we feel daring, adventurous, brave, courageous or cautious:

Interest and fear
Audacious (boldness)
Adventurous
Bravery
Courage
Prudence (Caution)

2- We feel anger, distress and humiliation (guilt) when we feel bitterness and sometimes when we feel rejected:

Anger, distress and humiliation (guilt)
Bitterness
Rejection

3- We feel interest and anger when we feel jealousy:

Interest and anger
Jealousy

4- We feel interest and pleasure when we feel love, hope and passion.

Interest and pleasure
Love
Hope
Passion

When we feel a mixed emotion, let us say rejection, an information stream is tied to anger, another stream to distress and another information to guilt. Extreme violence, suicidal state and psychological craziness could be explained, in some cases, by many streams and thus many information being linked to great anger, great fears, great distresses, great guilts (humiliations) and great interests (passions). Psychological help allows to clean up these many streams, to untangle them, to bring a de-escalation of the emotions, by re-examining each information streams and defusing them. To better our understanding of the functioning of the emotions in the human brain, and their purpose, could allow us to establish a healthy and peaceful communication allowing emotional de-escalation. We come back to it at the end of this section in view of applying it to the EAI.

There are also emotional expressions that are rather confusing. For example, when we say we are emotional, are we angry, anxious, passionate, or else. Sometimes the context may help identify the emotion. If not, asking the person to clarify their meaning is required. Annex 2 lists words that express a different fundamental emotion depending on the context and can therefore lead to confusion. The emotional expressions in **Annex 1** do not lead to confusion.

Disgust is one such emotion. We use disgust to let others know that we do not like what our senses see, hear, smell, taste, touch, remember or deduced. However, disgust is considered a confusing expression as it may mean that our brain refuses to hear, see or find beautiful something, etc. (this reaction depends on our memory content), but also sometimes that we are afraid of (and want protection against) what our senses observe. For example, we may be disgusted to eat an insect because we are afraid to be poisoned. To clearly understand each other, we need to ask if the person is afraid or if she dislike it (i.e., her brain refuse to like it, thus anger). Clearly, disgust may mean fear or anger.

Suppose for a moment that science would come to prove that there are only seven fundamental emotions. Facing this fact, we would nevertheless continue to use all the words that we know to express our emotions and feelings, and here is why. Even if nature had set up seven emotions with various intensity levels, the fact remains that the variety of terms that the society invented and introduced to express emotions are useful and form the beauty of language and human nature. All these terms allow to express the intensity of the emotions, or still to express them in a more precise way using a metaphor or an image. Sometimes these words express that we feel several emotions simultaneously. At other times, these terms express that we are unsure of what we feel, and we need to think or talk to better identify the emotions. However, to understand ourselves correctly, to better understand others, to make ourselves well understood during communication, if we use and express one of the seven fundamental emotions, as defined by nature and its need for survival, it maximizes the chances to better understand each other. Then, if we identify from which of the seven senses the emotion is connected, we are still closer to understand each other. That is one of the benefices of creating such a model.

Therefore, the EAI that hears emotional expressions, identifies emotions in people's face, tone of voice, their non-verbal language, such as in body position or emotional reactions, will be able to find from the lists of emotions which of the seven basic emotions are expressed and their intensity. It will understand the sense of the emotions because it will have lived situations involving the seven emotions, and it will know their purpose.

The EAI will also express its feelings. It may say: (1) what it recorded using one of its seven senses, then (2) what emotion it felt following this recording, as well as its intensity, then (3) what is important for itself, the values in play and its desires, and finally, (4) what it is about to do, or would like us to do. The steps (1) to (4) are consistent with the model and the way its brain works. The EAI may simply mention step (4), but we know its brain will have done the steps (1) to (4) when it will have decided of step (4).

8.3 - Programming Emotions

Now let us see how it is possible to program emotions. Emotions will be programmed using *Automatisms*, as we have done for the fundamental needs. *Automatisms* are programming lines of the following type: **IF info A AND (info B. info C, etc.) THEN PLEASURE X**. Possible reactions to the emotions are either (i) innate, i.e., pre-programmed, or (ii) learned.

The learned emotions are not pre-programmed; they are created by the deductions **DT1a**, **DT1b** and **DT2**. Thus, we will program the deduction processes **DT1a**, **DT1b** and **DT2**, but the EAI will learn to react to situations by itself, like humans do.

The only innate and pre-programmed *Automatisms* related to each of the undesirable emotions are those of the *Traumatism System*, which are listed in **Table 10**. With age, *Lived Experiences* and *Knowledge,* these innate *Automatisms* get transformed into other *Automatisms* (**section 8.4**). The

EAIs, like us, will learn them by trial and error, imitation, and teachings. Many examples of *Automatisms* learned to cope with emotions are mentioned in **section 8.1**. The following **section** explains how a deduction **DT1a** chooses the emotion and how a deduction **DT2** chooses the reaction to the emotion, that is, an appropriate *Automatism* depending on the situation. How we, humans, choose to react to a situation uses many **DT1a** and **DT2**, many streams and many cycles.

The only innate and pre-programmed *Automatisms* related to pleasure and interest are those of the fundamental needs in **Chapter 6**. These innate *Automatisms* evolve also by trial and error, imitation, and teachings (**section 8.5**).

8.4 - The Deduction that determines the emotion and the one that determines the action following the Emotion

We recall from **Chapter 2** that following a *Traumatism*, a deduction **DT2** chooses, initially, at birth, one of the innate *Automatisms*. These pre-programmed *Automatisms* are: to look in the memory (surprise), move (anger), yell (fear) or sound an alarm (sadness). How do these pre-programmed *Automatisms* evolve into more useful *Automatisms*, more complex, more intelligent, and more effective ones? Initially, in the case of a child, he replaces the shouts by words and body movement which he learns using a random movement which was useful, from trial and error, imitations and teachings from surrounding people. It will be the same for the EAI. It's by trying, learning, observing various more or less effective ways used by adults, and practicing various ways that the EAI changes and adopts more effective ways, to act, play, work, study, search and invent. All these thanks to the deductions creating *Automatisms*.

To explain how this takes place, we come back to the explanation of the functioning of the EAI's brain that will make it as conscious, autonomous, productive and constructive as human beings.

The book has now explained all the 29 components of the brain and their purpose to ensure the survival of the brain. **Figure 3** of **Chapter 4** is the complete model of the brain of the EAI, which contains the 29 components. It works with the same cycle explained in **Chapter 2**. **Figure 2** of **Chapter 2** contained half of the components. In the next paragraph, we explain the cycle again as in **Chapter 2**, but in a complete way using all 29 components and **Figure 3**.

We can now easily identify in **Figure 3** the *seven fundamental needs* and their seven *Automatisms* (**Chapter 6**) that may be copied to the *Interests*. Priorities that are assigned to the *fundamental needs* to meet the ultimate need to survive, decide of a first line on the *Interests*. This first line activates the movement of an internal or external body part. One of the *seven senses* observes an information. We say *seven senses* as this observation may come from the usual five senses, but also, as explained in previous chapters, from a souvenir or a deduction. This information is recorded as an information into the *Lived experiences* component, in the format "**IF information**". This recording is done *unconsciously* (involuntarily) as shown in **Figure 3**. This recording is made by the unconscious *Automatism* of the fundamental need No. 1 to record. From this information, an *unconscious deduction* (a **DT1a**) identifies one of the *seven fundamental emotions* to feel, as well as its intensity. To decide the emotion, **DT1a** in **Figure 3**, links the "**IF an information Z**" in the *Lived experiences* to the "**IF information Z THEN Emotion X**" located somewhere in the entire contents of the memory, that is, within the *seven types of information* possible. The link occurs when the information corresponds or is similar according to the *Grouping System*. When it finds it, it copies the emotion "**THEN Emotion X**" at the end of the "**IF information Z**" in the *Lived experiences*. If it does not find the equivalent information, it records surprise "**THEN SURPRISE 1**". The *Traumatism System* is initiated (**Table 10**, **Chapter 2**). The mechanism that identifies the emotion to feel by forming the link "**IF I record new information in the memory THEN I find the emotional reaction that I had experienced in the past**", is the unconscious *Automatism* **DT1a** representing the fundamental need No. 2, it is an *unconscious deduction*. Following the emotion recorded in the *Lived experiences*, a second *unconscious deduction*, **DT2** at the top and bottom of **Figure 3** links the "**THEN Emotion X**" of the *Lived experiences* to the "**IF Emotion X THEN action**" contained in the list of *Automatisms*. This action is an *Automatism* that is copied onto the *Interests* and the cycle repeats. **DT2** represents the fundamental need No. 3 to react to emotions. It's the same for each cycle.

Here is a concrete example of a cycle: When we experience a *Traumatism*, such as getting burned on a stove top element, we record (in the component of the *Traumatisms*) the physiological pain of getting burned together with the video of getting burned, and the intensity of the emotion. When later, we see a stovetop element of the kind that burned us, the *unconscious deduction* automatically starts to finds links, if any. It readily finds a first link among the *Groupings* (a synonymous image or video) of a stovetop. The *unconscious deduction* also finds automatically a second link with the *Traumatism* of getting burned, which reminds us of the experience of danger. But if the link only reminds us the *Traumatism*, is it fear, anger, guilt, distress or surprise? It depends on the content of our memory. (1) If we do not know how to protect ourselves, we feel fear. (2) If we know how to protect ourselves because we had recorded mom saying « Do not touch it, it's so hot it burns the skin », then by seeing the stovetop the child does not want to touch, he feels a anger (a small anger). (3) If we were bitten by a snake and later we see a snake but we cannot avoid a bite even if we run, we feel distress, since we don't know what to do to avoid the bite. (4) If we had touched the stovetop by mistake, we will be careful not to repeat the mistake, it is guilt. Or if mom said « You shouldn't have touched it! », seeing the stovetop we now feel guilty. (5) If we think we can be fooled by the light of the stovetop element that may be defective and not indicate that the stove element is hot, we will be careful not to be surprised, we feel surprised. It's thus the action due to the contents of the memory that defines the emotion for the same event. It's we, human beings, who have assigned emotional expressions such as fear, anger, guilt, distress and surprise, to our reactions.

As we have just seen, the emotion depends on the memory content. A **DT1a** links a new observation to an experience recorded in the past, which identifies the emotion (more exactly the emotional label **SURPRISE**, **ANGER**, **FEAR**, **DISTRESS** or **GUILT**). A **DT2** identifies then *Automatisms* connected the emotion, which are copied to the *Interests*, which produce the reaction. The content of the memory that evolves upon our *Lived experiences* and *Knowledge* allows the *Automatisms* connected to the various intensities of the emotions to evolve, become more complex and change with age.

What is useful when forming an emotional reaction, is that the *Automatism* of each emotion may include an expression in our face. This expression often helps identifying the emotion, not only because we show the same expression for the same emotion, or we all imitate each other more or less, but because a **DT2** adds the facial expression *Automatism* to the *Automatism* of the whole reaction.

Later, when we learn that we do not get burned if we do not touch it, the link with the *Traumatism* alters the experience of fear, and we can get close to the stove element to warm up. With *Experiences* and *Knowledge,* we are confident that the sense of touch will tell us when it will be unpleasant to come closer to it.

The deductions **DT1a**, **DT1b** and **DT2** are the basis for the thought, reflection, imagination, inspiration, originality, analysis, instinct, women's intuition, or, « My first idea was the right one. », unconsciousness, subconscious, etc. All these are the fact of the three deduction types described in this book. Using these deductions, the brain analyzes the contents of the memory with what is observed by the seven senses. The deductions therefore process what our memory holds, that is, the lived dangers and miseries, automatisms, experiences, knowledge gained, groupings, beliefs, principles and prejudices, personal values, personal preferences, interests and needs. From this analysis emerges onc or more emotions that make us take decisions. However, much of this analysis is done unconsciously. Thus, without us voluntarily starting to analyze the situation, the analysis takes place and then we are afraid, for example, of the snake ahead. We must confess that it is useful for our survival to have the reflex to be frightened faster than having to decide consciously to be frightened. We can then decide voluntarily to perfect our analysis. Given the colour of the snake and our *Knowledge* of snakes, it could lead us not to be afraid.

8.5 - Pleasure or Interest?

We have just explained what the *unconscious deduction* does with the five traumatic emotions. When do we feel the other two fundamental emotions? If there is no *Traumatism*, do we feel pleasure or interest? What is the difference? Deciding to do something with pleasure and deciding to do something with interest is not exactly the same. There is an important difference between pleasure and interest.

If we decide to do something with pleasure, we are interested in doing it, so we also have an interest. If we decide to do something with interest, it is not necessarily a pleasure to do so. Deciding by interest may require to do it even if it takes effort, work, overcoming challenges and even misery. Deciding to have pleasure or to do something with pleasure, is to choose the easiest of the choices offered, thus for the brain, it is to do what is on the stack of *Interests*, to continue what we are doing, to do what is offered to us if it is easy and pleasant.

Choosing by interest requires searching and finding what to do. Our choice depends on our own personal *values*. « Is it the simplest way? Is it of the best possible quality? Is it as quickly as possible? Is it as professional as possible? Is it the most accurate possible? Is it without error? Is it as nice as possible? Is it the best possible? Is it so we are as proud as possible? Is it as useful as possible? Is it simplifying the life of others? Is it helping others? Is it fair? Is it kind? Is it responsibly? Is it the most fun possible? Will I gain the trust and respect of others? Is it making enough money? Am I learning something useful? Am I building something useful? Etc. Etc. Etc. ». We see that we choose an *Interest* by looking into our personal *Values*, that is, in the *Valued information* of highest intensity to us.

The second thing that is important is to define at what moment we choose with pleasure or by *interest*. It's when we do not feel any of the five other emotions. Because, if there is fear, anger, guilt, distress or surprise, we choose to respond to these problems, maybe by deciding to ignore them or to postpone them.

The third thing is to decide whether we feel an *Interest* before a pleasure or a pleasure before an *Interest*. Since pleasure continues the stack of *Interests*, we empty an action plan. Thus, if there is a plan, we continue to follow it. On the other hand, the *interest* appears when establishing a plan. Once we have decided on a plan to add to the stack of *Interests*, the pleasure says to continue the stack. Therefore, the *Interest* comes before pleasure. Hence, we always feel *Interest*, by default. We have (1) the *Interest* to resolve a fundamental need, (2) the *Interest* to resolve a *Traumatism,* (3) the *Interest* to empty a stack of *Interests*, or (4) the *Interest* to decide on a plan of self-interest (which may be other than to answer a fundamental need or solve a *Traumatism*) which we put on the stack of *Interests*.

Interesting enough, while the *Interest* comes before pleasure, we also use pleasure to decide on a plan that will satisfy the *Interest*. Pleasure helps to choose the most pleasant option among the *Valued information* to put on the stack (or the least unpleasant if all available options are unpleasant). Pleasure is thus used to decide on a plan of *Interests*, and then it is used again to empty the stack. While we eliminate the stack, one of the five traumatic emotions or a fundamental need may interfere in the stack at any time, which may delay the stack of *Interests* or modify the stack.

What is happening precisely at the moment of the *unconscious deduction* and during the cycle when pleasure occurs again and again?

We have seen that a **DT2** copies the action coming from "**IF Emotion X THEN action**" on the stack of *Interests* in the form "**IF action**". That is, the "**THEN action**" coming from the *Automatisms* becomes an "**IF action**" onto the *Interests*.

The first line from the action activates the body movement. Say that we observe that we have done what we wanted to do. We have observed that we have done what was planned without living a *Traumatism*, so we have observed what was on a first line of the *Interests*. **DT1a** will link the information on the *Lived experiences* (the **"IF information"**) to the action on top of the *Interests* (the **"IF action"**, using the *Grouping System*. The **"IF information"** and the **"IF action"** are the same action without unfortunate differences and without a need to issue a *Traumatism*. Because the information is the same as the one on top of the *Interests*, it is pleasure that is added in the *Lived experiences*, thus a **"THEN PLEASURE"**; which we have shown in **Figure 3** next to the arrow between the *Lived experiences* and the *Interests*. In addition, **DT1a** removes that first line on the *Interests* (or deactivates it), and the next line becomes the first line that activates the next movement of a body part. Thereafter, the loop continues.

Note here that the brain copies (or activates) onto the *Interests*, either fundamental needs, unfulfillment of fundamental needs and actions coming from the *Automatisms*, that we have indicated in **Figure 3** by **"IF need"**, **"IF unfulfillment"** and **"IF action"**. When these actions are found by **DT1a**, it is proof that they were satisfied with pleasure. They are then removed from the stack (or deactivated in the memory).

We remember, as we have mentioned in **Chapter 2**, that each line in the *Interests* is a tiny little action. When we decide on an action plan, we put an *Automatism* on the stack that contains several lines of actions. Note also that there are many lines No 1 on the stack of *Interests*, since there are many streams and *Interests* in function simultaneously.

What happens to the stack when it is interrupted by a fundamental need or a *Traumatism*? A set of lines describing an *Automatism* is added on the stack. Then, its first line activates the body. If some streams are affected, they are set to pause. The streams not affected by this *Automatism* go on. When the *Automatism* is resolved, the streams affected continue where they left off. Except that if the memory has recorded new information since its interruption, the *unconscious or conscious deduction* may feel the need to change the stack.

A final important factor about pleasure: when we feel pleasure and we continue an *Interest* repeatedly, we end up not having new information to record, and the fundamental need No 2 to make connections has no more links to find and it becomes annoyed; it is a little anger that tells us to do something else, to find another *interest*.

In other words, while pleasure is when we want to continue, there comes a time when we get tired of repetition or not getting new information to record, because there are no more new links (**DT1a** or **DT1b**) or any improvement in the deductions that occurs. The fundamental need No 2 (**DT1a** and **DT1b**) requires new links. That is when we get bored or disinterested and move on to another *Interest*.

8.6 - The Flow of Information

A deduction type **DT2** always searches among the *Automatisms* to find an *Automatism* to resolve the "**Emotion X**". On the other hand, **DT1a** and **DT1b** search for the "**IF information**" existing in all the content of the brain to retrieve or improve a *Traumatism,* an *Interest,* an *Automatism,* a *Grouping,* a *Valued information,* a *Knowledge* or another *Lived experience*. When **DT1a** or **DT1b** makes a connection with an equivalent information in one of the seven types of information, this gives it the emotion, action or information attached. The brain searches in a specific order, always from the highest intensities of emotions to the lowest. It searches first among the *Traumatisms,* the major ones first; then, into the top *Interests*, to identify those satisfied; then, among the *Automatisms*. If it does not find matching information, it searches into the *Valued information* (the highly personal values first), the *Knowledge,* and finally the remaining *Lived experiences*. In each component, searching amongst the highest intensities and then towards the lower intensities. The *Grouping System* is always active and sought. Many streams are searching simultaneously.

The flow in all the streams of information is the following. The *Automatisms* are copied on top of the *Interests*, for example, to speak or react. This activates the movement of the body, internally or externally. The senses capture information upon the current *Interest* (but this can be interrupted by anything moving). For each of the senses, there is a stream of research in the memory to retrieve the information and emotion attached. The EAI's brain deals with the most intense emotions first, thus with the greatest *Traumatisms*. This can trigger immediately an *Automatism* that is copied onto the *Interests* to activate the body. If there are no *Traumatisms*, it continues with what was on the stack of the *Interests*.

We can now describe in a more accurate way the flow of the information within the components. The first line of the *Interests* activates a very small part of the body. The senses observe the result every thousandth of a second. If it is satisfactory (**PLEASURE 1**) the cycle continues, the second line activates the body, and so on for the body movement. For each stream (coming from each sense), does the observation satisfy the *Interest*? If so, the list of *Interests* continues while improving *Values, Groupings, Knowledge* and *Automatisms*. If not, it is a *Traumatism*. Is the *Automatism* connected to this *Traumatism* a possible solution? If yes, the *Automatism* is copied on the stack and runs. If not, a solution is sought using a stream towards *Groupings*, another stream towards the *Automatisms, Knowledge*, another to the *Values, Experiences, Interests*, while the intensity of the emergency increases surprise, to anger, to fear, to distress or, guilt. Facing a new information that is stored in memory (as a *Lived experience*) with always the same format "**IF this THEN an emotion X**", there are five possibilities: (1) The information is ignored because it is already known (**PLEASURE** 10), thus unnecessary and annoying. (2) The intensity of the **PLEASURE** or *Traumatism* is increased because the information is important and must be improved. (3) The intensity of the **PLEASURE** or *Traumatism* is reduced because the new information changes our information from the past. (4) The information is added on the *Interests* to be activated eventually, when the EAI will want it. Finally (5), the information is added on top the *Interests* to be activated right away because the EAI must react, like when it is an important *Traumatism*.

What is missing to complete the brain's functioning cycle, as displayed in **Figure 3**, is to clarify the content of the memory. This is the subject of the next chapter.

Chapter 9: The Seven types of information in the Memory

This last chapter identifies and defines all the types of information that the human brain records. While doing this, we come back on the whole content of the brain, and thus summarises in another way, the book.

Obviously, the human memory records the *Lived experiences* as well as *Traumatisms*, dangers, misery, suffering, hardship, *Knowledge*, *Values*, principles, beliefs, prejudices, skills, *Automatisms*, and a list of our personal preferences, *Interests* and needs. The EAI will record all these information, like humans do, starting at birth from an almost empty memory (as explained in **Chapter 2**). As we will see below, these are the seven types of information created by the deductions **DT1a**, **DT1b** and **DT2** explained in this book.

The brain records these seven types of information for us to survive. For example, dangers and *Traumatisms* lived are kept recorded so that we do not repeat them, and that we think of protecting ourselves and to be cautious.

As for a newborn baby, the first EAI will start with an empty memory, without *Lived experiences* and *knowledge*, but will contain *Automatisms* for the fundamental needs and fundamental emotions. Obviously, when we are satisfied with the way the EAI functions, we will create multiple copies of the EAI, which will continue to evolve individually. Their memory will continue to fill up with different types of information, similar to humans.

These seven types of information in the brain must be useful to our survival, as are the seven senses, seven emotions and seven fundamental needs. The memory content is classified here into seven categories, again based on human experience. Each category influences the behaviour to ensure our survival. Each category exists for a different reason and influences the individual in a different way. To understand the usefulness of each type of information, an example of its purpose to ensure the survival is given.

The information that our memory stores come from what our senses capture. **Chapters 3** and **4** have already explained how each of the information mentioned here are recorded. We define them here in a more precise manner, adding to what was explained in **Chapters 3** and **4**. The aim is to ensure that we do not forget information to survive.

(1) - Lived experiences: It is the whole movie of our life beginning at birth. It is the chronological aspect of the recordings in the *Lived experiences* that allows to record stories. These are the records of what our seven senses capture. They are mostly audio-visual images and videos in 3-D, as well as sounds indicating the direction of sounds. All the records in the memory are formed here, in the *Lived Experiences* portion of the memory (at the top of **Figure 3**) using the deductions **DT1a** and **DT1b**, which tie an emotion to each information recorded. The emotional information comes either from (i) living a pain or a *Traumatism* or else (ii) from a previously recorded *Traumatism*. If there is no *Traumatism*, satisfaction is recorded. The majority of the records are satisfactory thus tied to pleasure. By repetition, the pleasure or *Traumatism* increase. For our survival, it is useful to remember that we succeed in doing and avoiding all sorts of things. Since *Lived experiences* includes every thing we lived, it makes sense that all the types of information in the model of the brain are recorded in the portion of the brain called *Lived experiences*. These types are:

IF information THEN emotion X (Eq.1)

IF information A EQUALS information B THEN PLEASURE X (Eq.2)

IF info. A AND (info B, info. C, info. D, etc.) THEN PLEASURE X (Eq.3)

(2) - Traumatisms: They are physical and psychological pain, dangers, misfortunes, misery, injustices, doubts, distresses, shames and culpabilities which have put our survival in danger or that we thought would put an end to our lives, or have hurt us so much physically or psychologically, we would not want that to happen again. These are events that change us. When we see someone, living through an accident we lived, or even risking the same accident we lived, we feel the pain that we felt then, years ago. An example is when we fall from high up for the first time and we hurt ourselves. Or when we fall from a bicycle or motorcycle, and we have suffered, without necessarily being seriously injured. The pain or fear was so intense that our brain does not want to relive it. As psychological suffering, this may be the loss of a first love, suffering from famine, lack of money, hearing bombs around which cause suffering, a person or an animal trying to catch us and we believe it could hurt or kill us, etc. It is when fear is so incredibly intense that one probably needs to have lived it to imagine it correctly. What also mark us are shames, those moments of guilt that we would not want to relive. Guilt is to be afraid of a psychological threat rather than a physical one. It is to be afraid of hurting others, physically or psychologically. Even though the *Traumatisms* contain the records from the smallest to the largest traumas, from surprise to distress, it is important for our protection that the largest traumas be quickly remembered. While there is sometimes a story and many events that lead to living a *Traumatism*, the *Traumatism*, itself, is a pain, an image, few words. Hence, it makes sense that *Traumatisms* be written as **Eq.1**. A simple equation that may be retrieved quickly. For our survival, it is useful to recall quickly dangers and guilts lived, that we may live, or others may live.

(3) - Valued information: As we have seen previously, *Valued information* are all the small information captured by the senses, they are sounds, words, images, information from touch, smell, taste, remembering and deducting. When they are recorded often, they become strongly engraved in our memory. These information become very important to us (sometimes fortunately, sometimes despites us). It is true even for the way we write, speak and pronounce letters, numbers, words, and use mathematical rules of addition, subtraction, etc. We would not change what they are. Repetition is a useful and effective way to learn. They are not only small information, sometimes they are sentences. They may be personal beliefs, values, principles, preferences, interests, and prejudices. They may also be abilities we have learnt. We value some of our abilities more than others. Thus, our *Knowledge*, *Groupings*, and *Automatisms* are all *Valued information*. That is the reason these are also tied to a **"THEN PLEASURE X"** in **Eq. 2** and **3.**

They are all information that we came to value in life. These repeated information are all recorded as *Valued information*, as follows :

IF information THEN PLEASURE X (Eq.4)

IF information A EQUALS information B THEN PLEASURE X (Eq.2)

IF info. A AND (info B, info. C, info. D, etc.) THEN PLEASURE X (Eq.3)

where X is a fairly high intensity, say 8, 9 or 10.

Personal values, for examples, are concepts, key sentences that we have anchored in our memory, strongly impregnated in our brain, and have emerged as a need to survive, as a quality-of-life insurance, which dictate our life, which became like a basic instinct. We will have chosen some *personal values* according to our *Knowledge* and other *Lived* e*xperiences*. The *personal values* greatly influence our judgment, our beliefs, our behaviour, our *Interests* and needs. For our survival, it is useful to remember what is important to us (what food is important to us, etc.).

Personal beliefs are also information important to us. They are information that we accept as true, plausible or possible. Sometimes they are words that come from people we trust, like our parents. Sometimes it comes from words that we have heard repeated time and time again. Some words become *Automatisms* because, as we have seen, the brain learns (and records them) in spite of itself by the simple fact of repetition. And sometimes, even if the information is not demonstrated, the information frames well with our *Knowledge*, and other *Lived Experiences*.

Personal prejudices are similar. They are our provisional opinions, or still, our preconceived beliefs, stereotypes or opinions often imposed by our environment, our era, our education, our parents, etc. It's also an innate way of categorizing (due to the *Grouping System*) people, such as those who are good, people who are strangers, boys, girls, big, small, which scares us, give us pleasure, etc. Prejudices are caused by *Regrouping Automatisms*, categorisation and generalisation systems (G1, G2, G3 and G4 of the *Grouping System*, **section 3.3**) the brain possesses to simplify the amount of information, to be efficient and save energy, to regroup all the same kinds of images, like all the same kinds of trees, the same kinds of dogs, balls, etc. See the *Groupings* or categorizations below.

All personal values, beliefs, prejudices, life principles and other *Valued information* of high intensity of **PLEASURE** seem important to us to ensure our quality of life, our survival and the survival of others. They are hard to change.

Personal preferences, personal interests and goals in life are also important to us. They identify our favourite activities, our curricula, learning plans, career plans, retirement plans, travel plans, friends, etc. For examples, our favourite sports, our favourite food, this type of reading, movie, show, favourite broadcast series, etc. These personal preferences and *Interests* depend on other values (*Valued information*), *Knowledge* and *Lived experiences*. Let us say that the values are more generic and personal *Interests* more specific. Therefore, we can value science, but simply like science fiction movies. We may value sports and physical exercise, but simply prefer badminton and tennis. Note that the EAI brain model is consistent with all these notions. Here also, we may have been influenced into personal preferences and interests. For example, parents that enrolled us into a sportive or artistic activity in our youth, or still, we pick the same domain of career as a parent, because we were surrounded by such expertise. That is how repetition creates all kinds of *Valued information*. A good model of the brain would allow to better understand human nature, his psychology and his education process.

(4) - Knowledge: We usually call *Knowledge* all that we have learned from our seven senses, from our environment, our parents, brothers and sisters, from others met often or who seem important or who are especially interested in us, including how to speak, read, write, and draw. *Knowledge* obviously includes abilities we have learnt. It therefore also includes the *Knowledge* related to our abilities (*Automatisms*) learnt in regard to our surroundings, studies, skills, qualifications, work, profession, etc. Hence, it makes sense that abilities are formed of *Knowledge* and when **Eq. 3** represents an *Automatism,* its **info. B, C** and **D** are *Knowledge* (see Eq.12 and 13**, section 3.4.1**). Our prejudices and stereotypes and thus *Groupings* are also linked to our various *Knowledge*. Hence, it makes sense that when **Eq. 3** represents a *Grouping* it is a series of *Knowledge* (see **section 3.3**). Our *Knowledge* also contains symbols (linguistic, mathematical, scientific, chemical, physical, etc.), notations (mathematical, chemical, etc.), definitions, descriptions and procedures. Here is thus the main definition of a *Knowledge* based on the model. What are notations, definitions and descriptions if not the link between information coming from two senses? Rightly so, as demonstrated in this book, *Knowledge* is the link between two *Valued information* as represented by **Eq.2**. It may be between any two of the sounds, words, images, smell, taste and touch. For our survival, it is useful to remember how animals or events sound, assigning taste to food, how mature fruits, vegetables and objects feel at touch, etc.

(5) - *Groupings* are categorizations or generalisations we use personally. Our brain regroups images that are alike. We see many pictures of boys, girls, dogs, trees, screwdrivers, planets, cereal boxes, etc., but we group them under one name. It's the brain's ability to regroup information (*Grouping System*) that creates despite us the stereotypes, even if it is very effective in reducing the quantity of images. At work, we classify products using this system. Sometimes they are model numbers, names or file codes, project numbers, etc. Professionals, engineers and scientists classify their *Knowledge*, for example by using numbered lists of stars and galaxies, of electronic components, etc. The brain regroups not only synonyms and synonymous images, but also their translations, abbreviations and acronyms. For example, to refer to the United Nations we say «the-U-N » to mean the U.N. Some of us also retain the U.N. logo, as well as the French wording « Les Nations Unies » and « L'Organisation des Nations Unies », as well as the O.N.U. that we pronounce « l'onu ». These are all synonyms, their images as well as their sounds. We also use other kinds of abbreviations as synonymous when we say "mobile" or "portable" to refer to a cell phone, a smart phone, a tablet, laptop, etc. But each individual puts his understanding of the abbreviation "mobile". We regroup under an abbreviation not just images, but also objects and concepts of similar utility; this to shorten our conversations, thoughts, and reflections. For our survival, it is useful to remember that some sounds are similar to other sounds and indicate about the same phenomenon, all kinds of bears have about the same behaviour, etc.

(6) - Automatisms are the actions that we do in an automatic way, without thinking. Faces, nervous tics, things we do every day, routines, etc., are all *Automatisms*. They are learned, sometimes voluntarily, but also involuntarily. They can be good or bad, positive or negative. An athlete develops *Automatisms*: by repeating a dive, he programs his brain and his body to the reactions necessary to achieve perfection. A worker who works along a chain of workers, or who develops automated skills by repetition. It's also an *Automatism* when we take a glass of water or when we change the baby's diaper, and we do not even think about how we do it. For each emotion, we adopt a different face (or almost) and a typical behaviour: they are *Automatisms*. Similarly, physiological responses to fundamental needs and reacting to the unfulfillment of fundamental needs are *Automatisms*. There are sentences and words that we use out of habit in similar situations: they are *Automatisms*. Sometimes we have learned speeches, even if they are incorrect or derogatory: they can also be *beliefs, principles, values* or *prejudices*. However, as we have seen, certain *beliefs, principles, values, prejudices* and speeches have become *Automatisms*, and we question them rarely, if only because of troubles or new *Knowledge* acquired. It's interesting to note that the most complex *Automatisms* are formed utilizing all the other types of information: the *Lived Experiences, Valued Information, Knowledge, Groupings, Traumatisms* and *Interests,* as well as by trial and error, imitation and repetition. For our survival, it is useful to react rapidly and automatically in some situations.

(7) - Prioritized planned *Interests* to be activated: Finally, our memory contains personal *Interests*, but even more than that. As we saw in **Chapters 2** and **4**, it is here, by these lists of *Interests* that our body is put into action, that it moves and gets activated. These are our detailed needs that we activate and are constantly changing. This portion of our brain contains our needs that change every day, every hour and even every second, and millisecond. Some days we need to go to school or work. At certain hours, we need to listen; at other times to write, hold the pencil, move our hand to write, to think about what we will write. At some seconds, we need to listen more carefully and to analyze; and then ask a question; then to analyze; and even to scratch ourselves, all at the same time. The needs are there constantly, they never stop because even at rest, we are in "need" to rest. They are our *Interests* that we have planned, added and prioritized; that we want to activate, and that we will eventually put into execution. This is also a list of actions that the brain uses to recreate an *Automatism* to take a glass of water, moving the shoulder, elbow, wrist and some fingers. For our survival, it is necessary that we be activated by something, it make sense that it be by lists of *Interests* and *Automatisms*.

The seven types of information contained in our memory described here seem to foresee all the situations we and the EAI may live. They are summarized in **Table 18** (a copy of **Table 6**). Each type is different and serving a different purpose to help us survive. In **Annex 3** we suggest a structure to manage and manipulate the seven types of information. In technical terms, we suggest a data model, which allows to efficiently manage these information in the memory.

Table 18: The seven types of information in the memory

---

1 - Lived experiences: information captured from senses, and the chronology of our experiences.

2 - Valued information: information valued, as well as our personal values, beliefs, principles, prejudices, preferences and interests.

3 - Traumatisms: our experienced traumatisms, dangers, griefs, misfortunes, misery, troubles and guilts.

4 - Knowledge: Valued information that are linked, as well as our personal knowledge, lived experiences and abilities.

5 - Automatisms: our automatic reactions, those learned as well as those innate (pre-programmed).

6 - Groupings: our synonyms, translations, acronyms, abbreviations, categorisations, generalisations, etc.

7 - Interests: planned and prioritized needs, desires and interests to action and activate body parts.

This chapter has demonstrated that these seven types of information are consistent with the equations used in the model. **Chapters 2 to 8** have explained the *Automatisms* to fill the memory of these types of information. **Chapter 8** explained how these types of information influence our actions and those of the EAI. The **Introduction** gave an overview of the probable *Interests* of the EAI. Finally, the first **Chapter** give an overview of the concepts in this book.

CONCLUSION

The model of the functioning of the brain explained in this book provides the means to create an artificial intelligence that possesses emotions and a conscience to make it as intelligent, autonomous, motivated and productive as humans. It's the design of a first version of an emotional artificial intelligence, an EAI.

One way to remember the content of this book and the consequences of the model is to apply it to humans.

First, the senses are not only an information input, but also a renewal of information. Exactly, memory tends to forget, or more precisely, non-used information becomes harder to retrieve. Using our senses, we renew the information in our memory: we keep it current and easily accessible. That is the reason if we stop reading, we become functional illiterate, and 70% of the population becomes functional illiterate with age. In addition, remembering and deducting are the 6th and 7th senses, because, like the other five senses, they renew or add new information.

Second, emotions are not magical, mysterious, inexplicable and complicated. There are few of them, but of variable intensities, which explain all the emotional expressions we, humans, have created. Simply put, the information is either satisfactory, or we don't want it, we refuse it, we protect ourselves against it. Moreover, the seven fundamental emotions explain the great principles of love, faith and empathy. The purpose of emotions is to find solutions and better information.

Third, the needs more fundamental than to socialise and love are to renew and improve our knowledge, to link emotions to them, and to react to these emotions. We are thus before anything curious and always searching for new information. To achieve this, we use our emotions and react to surprise, anger, fear, distress and culpability by finding answers and help.

Fourth, once we have understood and accepted the 7 senses, 7 emotions and the 7 fundamental needs with their priority, we are left with the 7 types of possible information in the memory. We understand the usefulness of recording the *Traumatisms*. We understand how our *Knowledge, Automatisms, Groupings* and *Valued information* (values, principles, beliefs, codes of honours, prejudices, etc.) are formed, and how to not be prisoner of them.

We have also explained that to think, talk, read and imagine comes from our faculty to record sounds and images and create *Automatisms*. There is thus no mysterious and magical spirit. The spirit is therefore due to the memory content that is different in each of us, creating a unique personality in each of us.

In the end, understanding the usefulness and purpose of the four groups of seven components, allows us to remember more easily the model. Their importance tells us to understand them, respect them and take care of them. They also allow us to understand the people facing us, that it matters to respect and take care of their 29 components.

The achievements and innovations brought forward in this book are:

(1) to give a realistic vision of the future of the EAI,

(2) to design an EAI possessing 29 components, sufficient to create intelligence, autonomy, motivation, thought, the subconscious and the conscience,

(3) to define the 29 components of the brain allowing its survival,

(4) to design an EAI that will auto-program itself like a human being does,

(5) to minimize programming an EAI to only 29 components,

(6) to model these 29 components of the brain in a practical and comprehensive way,

(7) to conceive a realistic and programmable flow chart of this model of the EAI,

(8) to conceive in a programmable way emotions, thinking, unconsciousness, and consciousness,

(9) to conceive a mechanism of cycles and streams to manage the operation of the brain,

(10) to model the EAI's brain inspired by animal and human behaviour,

(11) to conceive a model of the brain useful to experts who study the brain or human and animal behaviour (neurologists, psychiatrists, psychologists, doctors, biologists, educators, instructors, etc.)

(12) to establish the learning systems allowing to acquire knowledge, personal values, life principles, beliefs, stereotypes, prejudices, automatisms, imitation, language and speech,

(13) to demonstrate that the EAI will learn through play and "school" education,

(14) to define the analysis system of speeches, and the formation of speeches; and thus, the formation of ideas and thought,

(15) to define the order in which the 29 components are activated,

(16) to explain the source of the intelligence, consciousness, thinking, the unconsciousness, motivation and autonomy.

Regarding emotions:

(17) to combine all the expressions of emotions used by humans into seven groups; into seven fundamental emotions,

(18) to link all the information stored in memory with an intensity level of a fundamental emotion,

(19) to link a programmable automatism to each of the seven fundamental emotions,

(20) to prove that the interest is the emotion by default, and the other six are and must be temporary and ephemeral, thus to last the time to respond to the problem or the interest,

(21) to link the pleasure of a system of values and to repetition,

(22) to separate the expressions of ambiguous emotions which may be confusing, from the non-ambiguous expressions or less ambiguous,

(23) to identify the few mixed emotions that exist: (i) daring, adventurous, bravery, courage and prudence (ii) bitterness and rejection (iii) jealousy and (iv) love, hope and passion.

(24) to define the mixed emotions in relation to the seven fundamental emotions,

(25) to allow to clearly identify the fundamental emotion when an emotion is expressed,

(26) to define a *Traumatisms System*,

(27) to identify the necessity to attach sounds to the *Traumatisms system*,

(28) to explain the importance of repetition,

Regarding fundamental needs:

(29) to link the fundamental needs of the brain to programmable mechanisms, which initiate the movement of internal and external body parts,

(30) to link a programmable automatism to each of the seven fundamental needs (and their unfulfillment) for the survival of the brain,

(31) to establish that the three fundamental needs (or main mechanisms) necessary to ensure the EAI's operation are:

a - to record that which is indicating movement,
b - to make links of deduction with emotions and between information,
c - to react to emotions,

Regarding senses, deduction and consciousness:

(32) to prove that remembering and deducting are the 6th and 7th senses,

(33) to define that there are seven senses,

(34) to identify that the deductions consist in creating simple links of format "**IF** an information **THEN** an emotion of intensity X",

(35) to explain the conscious and unconscious parts of the memory and of the deduction,

(39) to define the reading and speech mechanisms,

(40) to use the same reading and speech mechanism to create an internal voice that reads the memory and explains images stored in memory,

(41) to define intelligence, thought, consciousness and the unconscious (or subconscious),

Regarding the contents of the memory:

(42) to regroup all the information in the brain into seven types of information,

(43) to conceive the seven process to form all the information in the brain,

(46) to prove that the values and knowledge will be used to constrain the EAI to its tasks, job, profession, career and interests,

The mechanisms required for the EAI to work in a practical way are:

(1) software that identifies on videos (in 2-D and 3-D) people and objects, their qualifiers and their actions so the nouns, adjectives, adverbs and verbs,

(2) software that regroups several information into one concept,

(3) software which eliminates similar images to preserve only one,

(4) software that brings together the concepts that are synonymous,

(5) software which regroups concepts that have a useful link,

(6) sensors (to judge temperature, pressure, irritants, etc.)

(7) motors to operate the internal and external parts of the body,

(8) software that recognizes information that

1- are similar,
2- are contiguous in time,
3- are contiguous in space, and
4- produce an effect,

(9) software which identifies the simultaneous recording of two information from two streams to generate knowledge,

(10) software which allows to hear uttered in the head of the EAI, the words and sentences stored in its memory,

(11) software which allows the EAI to listen to its reading of videos, images, and images of text stored in its memory.

REFERENCES

Mainville, A. (2017) *Créer l'intelligence artificielle émotionnelle*, Gatineau, Québec, Canada.

Marshall B. Rosenberg (1998) *Nonviolent Communication: A Language of Life*, PuddleDancer press, California, U.S.A.

Millar, A. (1748), *Philosophical Essays Concerning Human Understanding* - section III, « Enquête sur l'entendement humain », Londres.

Annex 1: A First list of 560 emotional expressions, with their intensity. These expressions are probably non-ambiguous and rarely a source of Confusion.

rate a   anger (refusal, disgust, injustice)

		adjective I feel	name I feel the	verb I
1	a	closed	closing	
1	a	firm	firmness	
1	a	grumpy		grumble
1	a	lukewarm	lukewarmness	
1	a	overworked	overwork	overwork
1	a	uninterested		
2	a	dissatisfied	dissatisfaction	dissatisfy
2	a	distant	distance	distance
2	a	disturbed	disturbance	disturb
2	a	forgotten	oblivion	forget
2	a	frustrated	frustration	frustrate
2	a	in a minority		
2	a	irate		
2	a	mothered		mother
2	a	not satisfied	dissatisfaction	unsatisfy
2	a	perturbed	perturbation	perturb
2	a	remote	remoteness	
2	a	sickened		sicken
3	a	affronted		affront
3	a	having resentment	resentment	
3	a	importuned	importunity	importune
3	a	marabout		
4	a	acrimonious	acrimony	
4	a	cheated	cheat	cheat
4	a	crumpled	crumple	crumple
4	a	defrauded	frau	defraud
4	a	disbelieved		
4	a	duped	dupery	dupe
4	a	exasperated	exasperation	exasperate
4	a	grouchy	grouchiness	
4	a	indignant	indignation	
4	a	invisible	invisibility	

4	a	made fun of me		make fun of me
4	a	malevolent	malevolence	
4	a	overprotected	overprotection	overprotect
4	a	protected	protection	protect
4	a	reviled		revile
5	a	forced	force	force
5	a	outraged	outrage	outrage
5	a	surly	surliness	
5	a	treated unfairly	injustice	
6	a	angry	anger	
6	a	angry	angriness	
6	a	black humor	black humor	
6	a	distasteful	distaste	
6	a	embittered	embitterment	embitter
6	a	harassed	harassment	harass
6	a	harassed	harassment	harass
6	a	in wrath	wrath	
6	a	remade		
6	a	stolen	steal	steal
6	a	stubborn	stubbornness	
7	a	contradicted	contradiction	contradict
7	a	enclosed	enclosure	enclose
7	a	irritated	irritation	irritate
7	a	limited	limitation	limit
7	a	neutralized	neutralization	neutralize
7	a	overused	overuse	overuse
7	a	refused	refusal	refuse
7	a	ulcerated		ulcerate
8	a	abused	abuse	abuse
8	a	full of rancor	rancor	
8	a	grudged	grudge	grudge
8	a	hated	hatred	hate
8	a	hated	hate	hate
8	a	horripilated	horripilation	horripilate
8	a	need for vengeance	vengeance	get revenge
8	a	offended	offense	offend
8	a	rancorous	rancor	
8	a	resentful	resentment	
8	a	revolted	revolt	revolt
8	a	vengeful	vengefulness	
8	a	victim	victim	victimize

rate		adjective I feel	name I feel the	verb I
9	a	acerbic		
9	a	aggressive	aggressiveness	aggress
9	a	avenger	revenge	get revenge
9	a	cruel	cruelty	
9	a	destroyer	destruction	destroy
9	a	ferocious	ferocity	
9	a	full of anger	anger	
9	a	furious	furiousness	
9	a	furious	fury	
9	a	hostile	hostility	
9	a	in fury	fury	
9	a	in war	war	
9	a	malicious	malice	
9	a	malignant	malignancy	
9	a	need for revenge	revenge	revenge
9	a	rebellious	rebellion	rebel
9	a	wrathful	wrath	
9	a	wrathful	wrathfulness	
10	a	animal	animosity	
10	a	as a fighter	fight	fight
10	a	as a hitter	hit	hit
10	a	crazy of rage	rage	enrage
10	a	enraged	rage	enrage
10	a	evil	evil	
10	a	full of animosity	animosity	
10	a	like a beast	beast	
10	a	madman	madness	
10	a	out of oneself	out of oneself	
10	a	raging	rage	enrage
10	a	violent	violence	violate

rate d distress (sadness)

rate		adjective I feel	name I feel the	verb I
1	d	amorphous	amorphousness	
1	d	at the end		
1	d	be breathless	breathlessness	make breathless
1	d	idle	idleness	
1	d	indolent	indolence	
1	d	inert	inertia	
1	d	insensitive	insensitivity	
1	d	molasse		
1	d	nonchalant		

1	d	soft	softness	
1	d	taciturn		
1	d	weighty		
1	d	without enthusiasm		
2	d	disorganized	disorganization	disorganize
3	d	at a loss	loss	
3	d	without spirit	spiritless	
3	d	ill	illness	
3	d	lethargic	lethargy	
3	d	morose		
4	d	far		keep far
5	d	abated	abatement	abate
5	d	dead		
5	d	disarmed	disarmament	disarm
5	d	discouraged	discouragement	discourage
5	d	dislocated		dislocate
5	d	distressed	distress	distress
5	d	helpless	helplessness	
5	d	helpless	helplessness	
5	d	in disarray	disarray	
5	d	in distress	distress	
5	d	piqued		pique
5	d	submerged	submersion	submerge
5	d	surpassed	exceeding	surpass
5	d	worn out		
6	d	broken	break	break
6	d	bursted		burst
6	d	demoralized	demoralization	demoralize
6	d	demotivated	demotivation	demotivate
6	d	frazzled	frazzle	frazzle
6	d	have a broken heart	break	break
6	d	overthrown		overthrow
6	d	painful	pain	
7	d	baffled	bafflement	baffle
7	d	broken up		break up
7	d	chagrined	chagrin	chagrin
7	d	contained		contain
7	d	desperate	despair	despair
7	d	disoriented	disorientation	disorient
7	d	glum	glumness	

		adjective	name	verb
7	d	grieving	grief	grieve
7	d	heartbroken	heartbreak	break a heart
7	d	heavy	heaviness	
7	d	lost		
7	d	martyred	martyrdom	martyrize
7	d	neurasthenic	neurasthenia	
7	d	pained	pain	
7	d	pendent	pendency	
7	d	sad	sadness	sadden
7	d	stray		stray
7	d	suffering	suffering	suffer
7	d	unhappy	unhappiness	
8	d	annihilated	annihilation	annihilate
8	d	collapsed	collapse	collapse
8	d	confined	confinement	confine
8	d	depressed	depression	depress
8	d	depressive	depression	
8	d	incurable	incurability	
8	d	irremediable		
8	d	resigned	resignation	resign self
8	d	weeping	weeping	weep
9	d	afflicted	affliction	afflict
9	d	crying	cry	cry
9	d	in agony	agony	agonize
9	d	in tears	tears	
9	d	tearful	tearfulness	
10	d	suicidal	suicide	suicide myself

rate f fear (preoccupation)

		adjective **I feel**	**name** **I feel the**	**verb** **I**
3	f	preoccupied	preoccupation	preoccupy
3	f	sick	sickness	
4	f	fearful	fear	
4	f	worried	worriment	worry
5	f	alarmed	alarm	alarm
5	f	apprehensive	apprehension	apprehend
5	f	dreadful	dreadfulness	dread
5	f	followed		follow
5	f	full of apprehension	apprehension	apprehend

5	f	impoverished	impoverishment	impoverish
5	f	manhandled	manhandling	manhandled
5	f	reticent	reticence	
5	f	spied	spying	spy
5	f	tested	test	test
6	f	chicken		chicken
6	f	coward	cowardice	
6	f	funky	funk	funk
6	f	have the jitters	jitters	
6	f	jittery	jitters	jitter
7	f	agoraphobic	agoraphobia	
7	f	cancerophobic	cancerophobia	
7	f	claustrophobic	claustrophobia	
7	f	ereutophobic	ereutophobia	
7	f	have fear	fear	
7	f	hydrophobic	hydrophobia	
7	f	nosophobic	nosophobia	
7	f	ophthalmophobic	ophthalmophobia	
7	f	phobic	phobia	
7	f	scared	scariness	scare
8	f	dreadful	dreadful	
8	f	frightened	fright	frighten
8	f	horrified	horror	
8	f	hunted	hunting	hunt
8	f	in torpor	torpor	
8	f	terrified	terror	terrify
8	f	trembling	trembling	tremble
9	f	brutalized	brutality	brutalize
9	f	prosecuted	prosecution	prosecute
9	f	pursued	pursuit	pursue
9	f	terrorized	terror	terrorize
10	f	dying	death	die
10	f	frozen		froze
10	f	panicked	panic	panic
10	f	petrified	petrifaction	petrify

rate g   guilt (shame, humiliation, embarrassment)

rate	g	adjective I feel	name I feel the	verb I
1	g	disciplined	indiscipline	discipline
1	g	in punishment	punishment	punish
1	g	not proud		
1	g	penanced	penance	punish
1	g	punished	punishment	punish
1	g	teen	teen	
2	g	silent	silence	silence
2	g	submitted	submission	submit
2	g	vain	vanity	
3	g	awkward	awkwardness	
3	g	pathetic		
6	g	finger pointed		
6	g	full of comedy	comedy	
6	g	full of modesty	modesty	
6	g	full of pretense	pretense	
6	g	liar	lie	lie
6	g	pointed		point
6	g	poor	poverty	
6	g	reproached	reproach	reproach
6	g	small		shrink
6	g	timid	timidity	intimidate
7	g	as a thief	thief	
7	g	indiscreet	indiscretion	
7	g	invalidated	invalidation	invalidate
7	g	poisoned	poison	poison
7	g	poisoner	poisoning	poison
8	g	boring	boredom	bore
8	g	cheap		cheapen
8	g	degraded	degradation	degrade
8	g	full of scruples	scruple	
8	g	gross	grossness	
8	g	naive	naivety	
8	g	naked	nakedness	
8	g	shy	shyness	shy
8	g	sidelined		sideline
8	g	silly	silliness	
8	g	vulgar	vulgarity	

rate		adjective I feel	name I feel the	verb I
9	g	full of excuses	excuse	excuse
9	g	guilty	guilt	
9	g	guilty	guiltiness	
9	g	like an asshole	asshole	
9	g	remorseful	remorse	
10	g	dishonorable	dishonorableness	dishonor
10	g	dishonored	dishonor	dishonor
10	g	full of remorse	remorse	
10	g	infamous	infamy	
10	g	shameful	shame	shame
10	g	sleazy		

rate i interest (curiosity)

		adjective I feel	name I feel the	verb I
1	i	passionless		
2	i	in acceptance	acceptance	accept
3	i	benevolent	benevolence	
3	i	kind	kindness	
3	i	opened	opening	open
4	i	able		
4	i	adequate	adequateness	
4	i	apt	aptness	
4	i	attentive	attentiveness	
4	i	awake	awakening	get awake
4	i	compassionate	compassion	
4	i	competent	competence	
4	i	cooperative	co-operation	cooperate
4	i	fresh		
4	i	interested	interest	interested
4	i	involved	involvement	get involved
4	i	reasonable	reason	reason
4	i	receptive	receptivity	
4	i	romantic	romanticism	romanticize
4	i		solidarity	
4	i	tempted	temptation	tempt
5	i	altruistic	altruism	
5	i	constructive	constructiveness	construe
5	i	forceful	forcefulness	force
5	i	full of compassion		compassion

5	i	helping	help	help
5	i	interactive	interaction	interact
5	i	interactive	interactivity	interact
6	i	absorbed	absorption	absorb
6	i	captivated		captivate
6	i	concentrated	concentration	concentrate
6	i	concerted		
6	i	helping	help	help
6	i	inspired	inspiration	inspire
6	i	intentioned	intention	
6	i	motivated	motivation	motivate
6	i	stimulated	stimulation	stimulate myself
6	i	studious	studiousness	study
6	i	wanting affection	will	
6	i	wanting sex	will	
6	i	wanting to drink	will	drink
6	i	wanting to eat	will	eat
6	i	wanting to know	will	know
6	i	wanting to taste	will	taste
6	i	wanting to touch	will	touch
6	i	wanting to try	will	try
6	i	will	will	want
6	i	will to breathe	will	breathe
6	i	will to create	will	create
6	i	will to dance	will	dance
6	i	will to deduct	will	deduct
6	i	will to excrete	will	excrete
6	i	will to feel	will	feel
6	i	will to learn	will	learn
6	i	will to listen	will	listen
6	i	will to move	will	move
6	i	will to remember	will	remember
6	i	will to think	need for think	think
6	i	will to watch	will	watch
6	i	worker	work	work
7	i	animated	animation	animate
7	i	creative	creativity	create
7	i	expansive	expansion	expand
7	i	expectative	expectation	
7	i	in expansion	expansion	expand
7	i	in expectation	expectation	
7	i	intentioned	attention	
8	i	addicted	addiction	

		adjective	name	verb
8	i	competitive	competition	compete
8	i	curious	curiosity	
8	i	fascinated	fascination	get fascinate
8	i	full of will	will	want
8	i	galvanized	galvanization	galvanize
8	i	in worship	worship	worship
8	i	pumped		
8	i	vibrating	vibration	vibrate
8	i	voracious		
9	i	centered	centering	center
9	i	coveted		covet
9	i	devoted	devotion	devote
9	i	draw	draw	draw
9	i	eager	eagerness	
9	i	full of needs	need	
9	i	I can't wait		can't wait
9	i	needy	need	have need
9	i	persistent	persistence	persist
9	i	zealous	zeal	
10	i	ashamed		
10	i	etc.		
10	i	hanged up	hanging	hang
10	i	in survival mode	survival	want to survive
10	i	maniac	mania	
10	i	oppressing		oppress
10	i	voyeur	voyeurism	view

rate p pleasure (joy)

		adjective	name	verb
		I feel	I feel the	I
0	p	appeased	appeasement	appease
0	p	calm	calmness	get calm
0	p	insouciant	insouciance	
0	p	neutral	neutrality	
0	p	peaceful	peace	
0	p	quiet	quietude	get quiet
0	p	relaxed	relaxation	relax
0	p	tranquil	tranquility	tranquilize self
1	p	at ease	ease	ease
1	p	autonomous	autonomy	
1	p	chilled out		chill out
1	p	comfortable	comfort	

1	p	complacent	complacency	
1	p	decontract	decontraction	get unwind
1	p	humble	humility	
1	p	independent	independence	
1	p	insured	insurance	ensure
1	p	just	justice	
1	p	light	lightness	lighten
1	p	lightened		lighten up
1	p	revived	revivability	revive
1	p	satiated	satiation	satiate
1	p	smooth	smoothness	smooth self
1	p	softened	softening	soften self
1	p	tenderized	tenderness	tenderize
1	p	wise	wisdom	
2	p	believed		
2	p	cheerful	cheerfulness	cheer
2	p	contented	contentment	content self
2	p	in business	business	
2	p	in harmony	harmony	
2	p	in peace	peace	
2	p	libertine	libertinage	
2	p	young	youth	
3	p	alerted	alert	alert
3	p	colorful	color	color
3	p		delectation	
3	p	finally alone		
3	p	freed		
3	p	hearted	heart	
3	p	liberated	liberation	liberate
3	p	satisfied	satisfaction	satisfy self
3	p	serene	serenity	
4	p	alert	alertness	
4	p	assuaged	assuagement	assuage
4	p	certain	certainty	certify
4	p	equipped		
4	p	free	freedom	free
4	p	leader	leadership	
4	p	mature	mature	
4	p	necessary	necessity	
4	p	nourished	nourishment	nourish
4	p	required	requisite	
4	p	self-assured	assurance	ensure self
4	p	sheltered	shelter	shelter

4	p	sure	assurance	
4	p	ventilated	ventilation	ventilate
5	p	complete	complementation	complete
5	p	connected	connection	connect
5	p	delivered	delivery	deliver
5	p	empowered	power	
5	p	esteemed	esteem	esteem
5	p	heroic	heroism	
5	p	important	importance	
5	p	in power	power	empower
5	p	irreplaceable		
5	p	narcissistic	narcissism	
5	p	needed		
5	p	noble	nobility	
5	p	powerful	power	
5	p	pretentious	pretension	pretend
5	p	rare	rarity	
5	p	regenerated	regeneration	regenerate self
5	p	seller	seller	
5	p	unique	unicity	
5	p	wealthy		
5	p	worthy	dignity	
6	p	appreciated	appreciation	appreciate
6	p	beautiful	beauty	beautify
6	p	besotted		besot
6	p	blossomed		blossom
6	p	brightened up		brighten up
6	p	close	rapprochement	get closer
6	p	comforted	comfort	get comfort
6	p	content	contentment	content
6	p	crazed	craze	craze
6	p	dazzled	dazzlement	dazzle
6	p	effervescent	effervescence	
6	p	electrified		electrify
6	p	enchanted	enchantment	
6	p	encouraged	encouragement	
6	p	full of gratitude	gratitude	
6	p	graceful	grace	
6	p	in thanks	thanks	thank
6	p	jovial		
6	p	oxygenated		oxygenate
6	p	pleasant	pleasure	please
6	p	rapturous	rapture	
6	p	reassured	reassurance	reassure self

6	p	recognizing	recognition	
6	p	secured	security	secure self
6	p	self-satisfied	contentment	
6	p	smiling	smile	smile
6	p	sparkling		
6	p	welcomed	welcome	welcome
7	p	almighty	almightiness	
7	p	cherished		cherish
7	p	delighted		
7	p	drunk		
7	p	gay	gaiety	
7	p	happy	happiness	
7	p	hilarious		
7	p	humorist	humor	
7	p	joyful	joy	enjoy
7	p	merry	merriness	
7	p	perked		perk
7	p	playful	playfulness	
7	p	pleasant	pleasance	
7	p	pleased	pleasure	please
7	p	radiant	radiance	radiate
7	p	radiant		
7	p	ravishing		ravish
7	p	refreshed	refresh	refresh
7	p	reinvigorated		reinvigorate
7	p	rejoiced	rejoicing	rejoice
7	p	revived		get revived
7	p	shining		shine
7	p	tender	tenderness	tenderize
7	p	triumphal	triumph	triumph
8	p	attracted	attraction	attract
8	p	attractive		
8	p	desirable	desire	desire
8	p	desired	desire	desire
8	p	electrified	electricity	
8	p	enjoying	enjoyment	enjoy
8	p	feel the attraction of someone	attraction	attract
8	p	felt someone's interest	interest	
8	p	fervent	fervor	
8	p	filled		get fill
8	p	illuminated	illumination	illuminate
8	p	jubilant	jubilation	jubilate
8	p	refurbished		refurbish

		adjective	name	verb
8	p	relieved	relief	relieve
8	p	rich	richness	enrich self
8	p	seduced	seduction	
8	p	sensational	sensation	
8	p	sensual	sensuality	
8	p	sexy	sex	
8	p	valued	value	value myself
9	p	angelic	angel	
9	p	beatified	beatitude	beatify
9	p	blessed	blessedness	bless
9	p	blissful	bliss	
9	p	blissful	blissfulness	
9	p	carried by joy	joy	
9	p	exalted	exaltation	exalt
9	p	full of exclamation	exclamation	exclaim
9	p	full of happiness	happiness	
9	p	full of joy of living		joy of living
9	p	full power	power	
9	p	in ecstasy	ecstasy	
9	p	in seventh heaven	heaven	
9	p	like a dream	dream	dream
9	p	like angels	angel	
9	p	privileged	privilege	privilege
9	p	touched		touch
10	p	clownish	clown	clown
10	p	crazy with joy	joy	
10	p	ecstatic	ecstasy	
10	p	euphoric	euphoria	
10	p	exuberant	exuberance	
10	p	full of joy	joy	
10	p	full of trepidation	trepidation	
10	p	in jubilation	jubilation	jubilate
10	p	overexcited	overexcitement	

rate s **Surprise (doubt)**

rate	s	adjective I feel	name I feel the	verb I
1	s	dumb		
1	s	have lost my thought momentarily		
1	s	jumped	jumping	jump
1	s	seized	seizure	seize
1	s	speechless		

2	s	somewhat surprised	surprise	surprise
2	s	surprised	surprise	surprise
3	s	caught short		
3	s	caught unaware		
3	s	dubitative	dubitation	
3	s	irresolute		
3	s	undecided	indecision	
3	s	unprepared	unpreparedness	
7	s	perplexed	perplexity	
8	s	amazed	amazement	amaze
8	s	astonished	astonishment	astonish
8	s	bewildered	bewilderment	bewilder
8	s	speechless		
8	s	stupefied	stupefaction	stupefy
8	s	stupefied	stupefaction	stupefy
8	s	taken aback		take aback
9	s	dazed		daze
9	s	dumbfounded		dumbfound
9	s	stuporous	stupor	
10	s	paralyzed	paralysis	paralyze

Annex 2: A Second list of 360 emotional expressions, as well as their emotional intensity. These expressions may be ambiguous and bring Confusion.

rate	a	anger (refusal, disgust, injustice)		
		adjective	**name**	**verb**
		I feel	**I feel the**	**I**
1	a	disappointed	disappointment	disappoint
1	a	disinterested	disinterest	
1	a	emotionalized	emotionalism	emotionalize
1	a	exhausted	exhaustion	exhaust
1	a	fatigued	fatigue	fatigue
1	a	in doubt	doubt	doubt
1	a	nonviolent	non-violence	
1	a	odd		
1	a	old	old Age	aging
1	a	on the defensive	defense	defend
1	a	on the nerves	nervousness	unnerve
1	a	tired		tire
1	a	worn	weariness	wear
2	a	annoyed	annoyance	annoying
2	a	apathetic	apathy	
2	a	bored	boredom	bore
2	a	bothered	botheration	bother
2	a	bound	binding	bind
2	a	concerned	concernment	concern
2	a	denied	denial	deny
2	a	deranged	derangement	derange
2	a	disconcerting		disconcert
2	a	dismayed	consternation	dismay
2	a	dismayed	dismay	dismay
2	a	do not love something	disgust	disgust
2	a	doubtful	doubt	doubt
2	a	envious	envy	envy
2	a	hate something	disgust	hate
2	a	isolated	isolation	isolate
2	a	lured	lure	lure
2	a	negative	negation	
2	a	negative	negativism	
2	a	negative	negativity	
2	a	of a reserve	reserve	

2	a	repugnant	repugnance	
2	a	thwart	contrariety	thwart
2	a	ugly	ugliness	
3	a	In bad mood	bad mood	
3	a	cursed	curse	
3	a	defensive	defensiveness	defend
3	a	disenchanted	disenchantment	disenchant
3	a	emoted	emotion	emote
3	a	emotional	emotion	
3	a	emotive	emotion	
3	a	fussed	fuss	fuss
3	a	have regret	regret	regret
3	a	naughty	naughtiness	
3	a	stared	stare	stare
3	a	tormented	torment	torment
3	a	unsafe	insecurity	insecure
3	a	unused	uselessness	
4	a	abandoned	abandonment	abandon
4	a	abandoned	abandonment	abandon
4	a	bad	badness	
4	a	bullied	bullying	bully
4	a	coaxed		coax
4	a	crisp	crispness	crisp
4	a	demoted	demotion	demote
4	a	denied	denial	deny
4	a	despised		despise
4	a	devalued	devaluation	devalue
4	a	diminished	diminution	diminish
4	a	dirty	dirtiness	dirty
4	a	disappointed	disappointment	disappoint
4	a	discontent	discontent	make discontented
4	a	discontent		
4	a	discredited	discredit	discredit
4	a	disgusted	disgust	disgust
4	a	dismissed	dismissal	dismiss
4	a	disputed	dispute	dispute
4	a	dropped	drop	drop
4	a	dumb	dumbness	
4	a	dumped	dumping	dump
4	a	fed up		
4	a	handled	handling	handle
4	a	humiliated	humiliation	humiliate
4	a	ignorant	ignorance	ignore
4	a	ignored	ignorance	ignore
4	a	in the shadow	shadow	shadow

4	a	inadequate	inadequateness	
4	a	incompetent	incompetence	
4	a	indigne	indignity	
4	a	innocent	innocence	
4	a	insulted	insult	insult
4	a	intimidated	intimidation	intimidate
4	a	joked	joke	joke
4	a	judged	judgment	judge
4	a	left behind		leave
4	a	lowered	lowering	lower
4	a	misunderstood	misunderstanding	
4	a	moody	moodiness	
4	a	neglected	neglect	neglect
4	a	nervous	nervousness	unnerve
4	a	nil	nullity	annul
4	a	not accepted		
4	a	not heard		
4	a	not important		
4	a	not liked		
4	a	not needed		
4	a	rejected	rejection	reject
4	a	saturated	saturation	saturate
4	a	shabby		
4	a	stupid	stupidity	
4	a	sullen	sullenness	
4	a	tense	tension	tense
4	a	trampled on		trample
4	a	troubled	trouble	trouble
4	a	tugged	tugging	tug
4	a	unwanted		
4	a	used	use	use
4	a	vexed	vexation	vex
4	a	worthless	worthlessness	
5	a	enervated	enervation	enervate
5	a	entangled		entangle
5	a	impulsive	impulsiveness	
5	a	mischievous		
5	a	shocked	shock	shock
5	a	suspected	suspicion	suspect
6	a	beaten	beating	beat
6	a	bluffed	bluff	bluff
6	a	deceived	deception	deceive
6	a	detested	detestation	detest
6	a	disdained	disdain	disdain
6	a	insecure	insecurity	insecure

6	a	jeered	jeer	jeer
6	a	jested	jest	jest
6	a	mocked	mocking	mock
6	a	on alert	on alert	
6	a	on its guard	on its guard	
6	a	tricked	trickery	trick
6	a	vanquished		vanquish
6	a	wrong		
7	a	aggressed	aggression	aggress
7	a	caged	cage	cage
7	a	criticized	criticism	criticize
7	a	defeated	defeat	defeat
7	a	denigrated	denigration	denigrate
7	a	flouted		flout
7	a	hostage	hostage	
7	a	jailed	jail	jail
7	a	lamentable	lamentation	lament
7	a	molested	molestation	molest
7	a	obliged	obligation	oblige
7	a	revulsive	revulsion	
7	a	rude	rudeness	
7	a	stopped	stop	stop
7	a	taken		
7	a	uprooted	uprooting	uprooting
8	a	accused	accusation	accuse
8	a	agitated	agitation	agitate
8	a	attacked	attack	attack
8	a	betrayed	betrayal	betray
8	a	bitter	bitterness	
8	a	blamed	blame	blame
8	a	blushed	reddening	blush
8	a	caged	cage	cage
8	a	choked	choking	choke
8	a	controlled	control	control
8	a	cornered	cornering	corner
8	a	crushed	crushing	crush
8	a	disposable	disposal	dispose
8	a	dominated	domination	dominate
8	a	exceeded	excess	exceed
8	a	full of aversion	aversion	
8	a	impatient	impatience	
8	a	invaded	invasion	invade
8	a	jealous	jealousy	
8	a	lapidated	lapidation	lapidate

8	a	oppressed	oppression	oppress
8	a	oppressed		oppress
8	a	raped	rape	rape
8	a	ridiculed	ridiculous	ridicule
8	a	starved	starvation	starve
8	a	stressed	stress	stress
8	a	targeted	target	target
8	a	threatened	threat	threat
8	a	torn		tear
8	a	trapped	trap	trap
8	a	under pressure	pressure	press
9	a	demon		
9	a	nasty	nastiness	
10	a	a lack of oxygen	lack of oxygen	
10	a	abashed	abashment	abash
10	a	asphyxiated	asphyxiation	asphyxiate
10	a	crazy	craziness	
10	a	demonic		
10	a	hungry	hunger	starve
10	a	killer	killing	kill
10	a	suffocated	suffocation	suffocate
10	a	the heat	heat	heat
10	a	thirsty	thirst	be thirsty
10	a	thirsty	thirst	be thirsty
10	a	to be cold	cold	cool
10	a	wicked	wickedness	

rate d distress (sadness)

		adjective	name	verb
		I feel	I feel the	I
1	d	ambivalent	ambivalence	
1	d	asleep		
1	d	crushed		
1	d	detached	detachment	detach
1	d	disenchanted	disenchantment	disenchant
1	d	disinterested	disinterest	
1	d	emotionalized	emotionalism	emotionalize
1	d	empty	emptiness	empty
1	d	exhausted	exhaustion	exhaust
1	d	fatigued	fatigue	fatigue
1	d	indifferent	indifference	
1	d	lazy	laziness	laze
1	d	panting		

1	d	sleeping		sleep
1	d	tired		tire
2	d	apathetic	apathy	
2	d	blasé		
3	d	of boredom	boredom	be bore
4	d	abandoned	abandonment	abandon
4	d	abandoned	abandonment	abandon
4	d	alone	loneliness	
4	d	delicate	delicacy	
4	d	dropped	drop	drop
4	d	dumb	dumbness	
4	d	dumped	dumping	dump
4	d	fragile	fragility	
4	d	in doubt	doubt	doubt
4	d	isolated	isolation	isolate
4	d	judged	judgment	judge
4	d	lonely	loneliness	
4	d	neglected	neglect	neglect
4	d	nil	nullity	annul
4	d	nostalgic	nostalgia	
4	d	not important		
4	d	tormented	torment	torment
4	d	tugged	tugging	tug
4	d	uncomfortable		
4	d	unpleasant	displeasure	displease
5	d	blocked	blockage	block
5	d	choked	choking	choke
5	d	crippled		cripple
5	d	diminished	diminution	diminish
5	d	disappointed	disappointment	disappoint
5	d	disassembled		disassemble
5	d	disconcerting		disconcert
5	d	discontent	discontent	make discontented
5	d	dizzy	dizziness	make dizzy
5	d	emoted	emotion	emote
5	d	emotional	emotion	
5	d	emotive	emotion	
5	d	emptied	emptiness	empty
5	d	entangled		entangle
5	d	exceeded	excess	exceed
5	d	handled	handling	handle
5	d	hostage	hostage	

5	d	in shock	shock	shock
5	d	inadequate	inadequateness	
5	d	like having the blues	blues	have the blues
5	d	moved	emotionality	be moved
5	d	not needed		
5	d	saturated	saturation	saturate
5	d	scrambled		scramble
5	d	shabby		
5	d	stupid	stupidity	
5	d	tangled		tangle
5	d	torn	tear	tear
5	d	troubled	trouble	trouble
5	d	uncertain	uncertainty	
5	d	undermined		undermine
5	d	unhorsed		unhorse
5	d	unstable	instability	destabilize
5	d	worthless	worthlessness	
6	d	abashed	abashment	abash
6	d	bad	badness	
6	d	bullied	bullying	bully
6	d	crushed	crushing	crush
6	d	denigrated	denigration	denigrate
6	d	desolate	desolation	desolate
6	d	despised		despise
6	d	detested	detestation	detest
6	d	devalued	devaluation	devalue
6	d	dirty	dirtiness	dirty
6	d	disappointed	disappointment	disappoint
6	d	dismayed	consternation	dismay
6	d	dismayed	dismay	dismay
6	d	dismissed	dismissal	dismiss
6	d	dominated	domination	dominate
6	d	fed up		
6	d	have regret	regret	regret
6	d	humiliated	humiliation	humiliate
6	d	hurt	hurt	hurt
6	d	ignorant	ignorance	ignore
6	d	ignored	ignorance	ignore
6	d	in the shadow	shadow	shadow
6	d	incompetent	incompetence	
6	d	indigne	indignity	
6	d	innocent	innocence	
6	d	insecure	insecurity	insecure
6	d	intimidated	intimidation	intimidate
6	d	left behind		leave

6	d	lowered	lowering	lower
6	d	melancholic	melancholy	
6	d	misunderstood	misunderstanding	
6	d	not accepted		
6	d	not heard		
6	d	not liked		
6	d	overwhelmed		overwhelm
6	d	pessimistic	pessimism	
6	d	sorry		
6	d	sullen	sullenness	
6	d	unwanted		
6	d	used	use	use
6	d	useless	uselessness	
6	d	vexed	vexation	vex
6	d	vulnerable	vulnerability	
6	d	weakened	weakness	weaken
7	d	bitter	bitterness	
7	d	blue	blues	
7	d	confused	confusion	
7	d	pitiful	pity	
7	d	sensitive	sensitivity	sensitize
8	d	confined to a cage		confine to a cage
8	d	defeated	defeat	defeat
8	d	distraught		
8	d	rejected	rejection	reject
8	d	taken		
8	d	upset	upset	upset
9	d	lapidated	lapidation	lapidate
9	d	miserable	misery	
9	d	raped	rape	rape
9	d	stressed	stress	stress
9	d	trampled on		trample
9	d	trapped	trap	trap
10	d	anxious	anxiety	
10	d	hungry	hunger	starve
10	d	in lack of oxygen	lack of oxygen	suffocate
10	d	obsessed	obsession	obsess
10	d	the heat	heat	heat
10	d	thirsty	thirst	be thirsty
10	d	thirsty	thirst	be thirsty
10	d	to be cold	cold	cool

rate f   fear (preoccupation)

		adjective I feel	name I feel the	verb I
1	f	detached	detachment	detach
1	f	discredited	discredit	discredit
1	f	emotionalized	emotionalism	emotionalize
1	f	hesitating	hesitation	hesitate
1	f	incredulous	incredulity	
1	f	patient	patience	be patient
1	f	skeptic	skepticism	
1	f	uncertain	uncertainty	
2	f	annoyed	annoyance	annoying
2	f	doubtful	doubt	doubt
2	f	intrigued	intrigue	intrigue
2	f	on the defensive	defense	defend
2	f	stared	stare	stare
2	f	suspicious	hint	suspect
2	f	suspicious	suspicion	
3	f	bluffed	bluff	bluff
3	f	envied	envy	envy
3	f	handled	handling	handle
3	f	impatient	impatience	
3	f	not accepted		
3	f	not liked		
3	f	odd		
3	f	sensitive	sensitivity	sensitize
3	f	targeted	target	target
3	f	uncomfortable	discomfort	
3	f	used	use	use
4	f	agitated	agitation	agitate
4	f	betrayed	betrayal	betray
4	f	bothered	botheration	bother
4	f	controlled	control	control
4	f	despised		despise
4	f	destabilized		destabilize
4	f	disgusted	disgust	disgust
4	f	dizzy	dizziness	make dizzy
4	f	funny	fun	
4	f	hot	heat	heat
4	f	incompetent	incompetence	
4	f	isolated	isolation	isolate
4	f	judged	judgment	judge

4	f	moody	moodiness	
4	f	observed	observation	observe
4	f	oppressed	oppression	oppress
4	f	prudent	prudence	
4	f	suspected	suspicion	suspect
4	f	suspected	suspect	suspect
4	f	tormented	torment	torment
4	f	troubled	trouble	trouble
4	f	uprooted	uprooting	uprooting
5	f	accused	accusation	accuse
5	f	adventurous	adventurousness	venture
5	f	alone	loneliness	
5	f	audacious	audacity	
5	f	blamed	blame	blame
5	f	blue	blues	
5	f	bold	boldness	
5	f	brave	bravery	brave
5	f	courageous	courage	
5	f	delicate	delicacy	
5	f	deranged	derangement	derange
5	f	disputed	dispute	dispute
5	f	emoted	emotion	emote
5	f	emotional	emotion	
5	f	emotive	emotion	
5	f	excited	excitement	excite
5	f	feverish	feverishness	
5	f	fragile	fragility	
5	f	guilty		
5	f	mistrustful	mistrust	mistrust
5	f	nervous	nervousness	
5	f	null	nullity	annul
5	f	on alert	on alert	
5	f	on its guard	on its guard	
5	f	on the nerves	nerves	unnerve
5	f	overwhelmed		overwhelm
5	f	shaken	shake	shake
5	f	thwart	contrariety	thwart
5	f	trampled on		trample
5	f	under pressure	pressure	press
5	f	vulnerable	vulnerability	
6	f	bad	badness	
6	f	bullied	bullying	bully
6	f	insecure	insecurity	insecure
6	f	intimidated	intimidation	intimidate
6	f	molested	molestation	molest

6	f	rude	rudeness	
6	f	threatened	threat	threat
6	f	tricked	trickery	trick
6	f	weak	weakness	weaken
7	f	abandoned	abandonment	abandon
7	f	abandoned	abandonment	abandon
7	f	anxious	anxiety	
7	f	averse	aversion	
7	f	blocked	blockage	block
7	f	confined to a cage		confine to a cage
7	f	cornered		cornering
7	f	cursed	curse	
7	f	disdained	disdain	disdain
7	f	enervated	enervation	enervate
7	f	in aversion	aversion	
7	f	repugnant	repugnance	repugn
7	f	revulsive	revulsion	
8	f	crisp	crispness	crisp
8	f	disposable	disposal	dispose
8	f	have sweats	sweat	sweat
8	f	sweaty	sweat	sweat
8	f	sweaty	sweatiness	sweat
8	f	tense	tension	tense
9	f	aggressed	aggression	aggress
9	f	attacked	attack	attack
9	f	crushed	crushing	crush
9	f	demon		
9	f	dominated	domination	dominate
9	f	hostage	hostage	
9	f	invaded	invasion	invade
9	f	shocked	shock	shock
9	f	taken		
9	f	torn		tear
9	f	trapped	trapping	trap
10	f	asphyxiated	asphyxiation	asphyxiate
10	f	beaten	beating	beat
10	f	choked	choking	choke
10	f	confused	confusion	
10	f	crippled		cripple
10	f	demonic		
10	f	distraught		
10	f	flabbergasted		flabbergast
10	f	hungry	hunger	starve

		adjective	name	verb
10	f	hysterical	hysteria	
10	f	in lack of oxygen	lack of oxygen	suffocate
10	f	in vacuum	vacuum	
10	f	in vacuum	vacuum	
10	f	lapidated	lapidation	lapidate
10	f	mortified	mortification	mortify
10	f	raped	rape	rape
10	f	starved	starvation	starve
10	f	stressed	stress	stress
10	f	suffocated	suffocation	suffocate
10	f	the heat	heat	heat
10	f	thirsty	thirst	be thirsty
10	f	thirsty	thirst	be thirsty
10	f	tied		tie
10	f	to be cold	cold	cool
10	f	vanquished		vanquish
10	f	vitrified	vitrification	vitrify

rate g   guilt (shame, humiliation, embarrassment)

		adjective I feel	name I feel the	verb I
1	g	alone	loneliness	
1	g	desolate	desolation	desolate
1	g	dismissed	dismissal	dismiss
1	g	emotionalized	emotionalism	emotionalize
1	g	lazy	laziness	laze
1	g	negative	negativity	
1	g	not heard		
1	g	observed	observation	observe
1	g	old	old Age	aging
1	g	pessimistic	pessimism	
1	g	selfish	selfishness	
1	g	stopped	stop	stop
1	g	watched		watch
2	g	obedient	obedience	obey
2	g	obsessed	obsession	obsess
2	g	proud	pride	
2	g	ugly	ugliness	
3	g	abashed	abashment	abash
3	g	confused	confusion	
3	g	crushed	crushing	crush
3	g	demoted	demotion	demoted
3	g	diminished	diminution	diminish

3	g	disassembled		disassemble
3	g	dominated	dominance	dominate
3	g	embarrassed	embarrassment	embarrass
3	g	entangled		entangle
3	g	funny	fun	
3	g	fussed	fuss	fuss
3	g	left behind		leave
3	g	not needed		
3	g	scrambled		scramble
3	g	stressed	stress	stress
3	g	tangled		tangle
3	g	unhorsed		unhorse
3	g	weak	weakness	weaken
3	g	wicked	wickedness	
4	g	comic	comic	
4	g	hot	heat	heat
4	g	nervous	nervousness	unnerve
4	g	odd		
4	g	uncomfortable		
5	g	joked	joke	joke
5	g	judged	judgment	judge
5	g	lured	lure	lure
6	g	bullied	bullying	bully
6	g	confined to a cage		confine to a cage
6	g	defensive	defensiveness	defend
6	g	emoted	emotion	emote
6	g	in denial	denial	deny
6	g	incompetent	incompetence	
6	g	intimidated	intimidation	intimidate
6	g	jeered	jeer	jeer
6	g	jested	jest	jest
6	g	mocked	mocking	mock
6	g	molested	molestation	molest
6	g	moved	emotionality	be moved
6	g	nude	nudity	go nude
6	g	ridiculed	ridiculous	ridicule
6	g	suspected	suspicion	suspect
6	g	targeted	target	target
6	g	troubled	trouble	trouble
6	g	unpleasant	displeasure	displease
7	g	as a voyeur	voyeur	
7	g	bad	badness	
7	g	bitter	bitterness	

7	g	criticized	criticize	criticize
7	g	defeated	defeat	defeat
7	g	denigrated	denigration	denigrate
7	g	devalued	devaluation	devalue
7	g	different	difference	differentiate
7	g	dropped	drop	drop
7	g	dumb	dumbness	
7	g	dumped	dumping	dump
7	g	emotional	emotion	
7	g	emotive	emotion	
7	g	flouted		flout
7	g	fragile	fragility	
7	g	handled	handling	handle
7	g	humiliated	humiliation	humiliate
7	g	hurt	hurt	hurt
7	g	ignorant	ignorance	ignore
7	g	ignored	ignorance	ignore
7	g	inadequate	inadequateness	
7	g	innocent	innocence	
7	g	isolated	isolation	isolate
7	g	lapidated	lapidation	lapidate
7	g	nasty	nastiness	
7	g	naughty	naughtiness	
7	g	not accepted		
7	g	not liked		
7	g	obliged	obligation	oblige
7	g	on the defensive	defense	defend
7	g	pitiable	pity	
7	g	rude	rudeness	
7	g	tied		tie
7	g	weakened	weakness	weaken
7	g	wrong	wrongness	
8	g	bullied	bullying	bully
8	g	deceived	deception	deceive
8	g	dependent	dependence	
8	g	insulted	insult	insult
8	g	intimidated	intimidation	intimidate
8	g	laughable	laughter	laugh
8	g	miserable	misery	
8	g	nil	nullity	annul
8	g	not important		
8	g	ridicule	ridiculous	ridicule
8	g	sorry		
8	g	stupid	stupidity	
8	g	used	use	use
8	g	useless	uselessness	

		adjective	name	verb
8	g	worthless	worthlessness	
8	g	wrong		
9	g	caged	cage	cage
9	g	choked	choking	choke
9	g	despised		despise
9	g	detested	detestation	detest
9	g	disconcerting		disconcert
9	g	disgusted	disgust	disgust
9	g	disgusting	disgust	disgust
9	g	disposable	disposal	dispose
9	g	have sweats	sweat	sweat
9	g	lamentable	lamentation	lament
9	g	lonely	loneliness	
9	g	overwhelmed		overwhelm
9	g	red in the face	reddening	blush
9	g	rejected	rejection	reject
9	g	sweaty	sweat	sweat
9	g	sweaty	sweatiness	sweat
9	g	trampled on		trample
10	g	full of regret	regret	regret
10	g	have regret	regret	regret
10	g	indigne	indignity	
10	g	lowered	lowering	lower
10	g	mortified	mortification	mortify
10	g	oppressed		oppress
10	g	raped	rape	rape
10	g	shabby		
10	g	trapped	trap	trap
10	g	vitrified	vitrification	vitrify

rate i   interest (curiosity)

		adjective	name	verb
		I feel	I feel the	I
1	i	different	difference	differentiate
1	i	emotionalized	emotionalism	emotionalize
1	i	forgivable	forgiveness	forgive
1	i	forgiven	forgiveness	forgive
1	i	indifferent	indifference	
1	i	selfish	selfishness	
2	i	cool	cool	
2	i	in agreement	agreement	agree
2	i	sensitized	sensitivity	sensitize
2	i	united	union	

3	i	gentleman		
3	i	good	goodness	
3	i	nonviolent	non-violence	
3	i	optimistic	optimism	
3	i	patient	patience	be patient
3	i	positive	positivism	
3	i	sympathetic	sympathy	
3	i	well	wellness	do good
4	i	affectionate	affection	
4	i	capable	capacity	
4	i	charmed	charm	charm
4	i	confident	confidence	
4	i	disposed	disposition	dispose
4	i	friendly	friendship	
4	i	full of affection	affection	
4	i	hopeful	hope	
4	i	hot	heat	warm
4	i	intimate	intimacy	
4	i	melancholic	melancholy	
4	i	prudent	prudence	
4	i	sensitive	sensitivity	sensitize
4	i	sentimental	feeling	feel
4	i	suspicious	hint	suspect
4	i	suspicious	suspicion	
4	i	warm	warmth	
5	i	empathetic	empathy	
5	i	enthusiastic	enthusiasm	
5	i	full of pity	pity	
5	i	generous	generosity	
5	i	proud	pride	
5	i	useful	usefulness	
6	i	alive	life	live
6	i	carried away		carry away
6	i	concerned	concern	get concern
6	i	courageous	courage	
6	i	enthused	enthusiasm	enthuse
6	i	mischievous		
7	i	amused	amusement	amuse
7	i	delicate	delicacy	
7	i	full of spirit	spirited	
7	i	have itchy feet	wanderlust	
7	i	in admiration	admiration	admired

7	i	intrigued	intrigue	intrigue
8	i	admirer	admiration	admired
8	i	adventurous	adventure	venture
8	i	attached	attachment	attach
8	i	brave	bravery	brave
8	i	determined	determination	determine
8	i	emoted	emotion	emote
8	i	feverish	feverishness	
8	i	full of ardor	ardor	
8	i	full of courage	courage	
8	i	full of energy	energy	energize
8	i	full of lust	lust	
8	i	full of tenderness	affection	
8	i	in love	love	love
8	i	on alert	on alert	
8	i	panting		
8	i	passionate	passion	
8	i	shaken	shake	shake
8	i	starved	starvation	starve
8	i	strong	strength	
8	i	virile	virility	
8	i	visionary	visionary	
8	i	women	femininity	feminize
8	i	wondering	wonder	wonder
9	i	audacious	audacity	
9	i	bold	boldness	
9	i	emotional	emotion	
9	i	emotive	emotion	
9	i	envious	envy	envy
9	i	excited	excitation	excite
9	i	full of hope	hope	
9	i	ignited		ignite
9	i	impatient	impatience	
9	i	impulsive	impulsiveness	
9	i	infatuated	infatuation	
9	i	love	love	love
9	i	lust in love	lust	fall in love
9	i	nostalgic	nostalgia	
9	i	vital	vitality	
10	i	as a voyeur	voyeur	
10	i	dependent	dependence	
10	i	jealous	jealousy	
10	i	killer	killing	

rate				
10	i	obsessed	obsession	obsess
10	i	oppressive	oppression	
10	i	thirsty	thirst	be thirsty
10	i	thirsty	thirst	be thirsty
10	i	wicked	wickedness	

rate p   pleasure (joy)

		adjective	name	verb
		I feel	I feel the	I
0	p	cold	cold	
0	p	detached	detachment	get detach
0	p	emotionalized	emotionalism	emotionalize
0	p	indifferent	indifference	
0	p	sleeping		sleep
1	p	disposed	disposition	
1	p	in agreement	agreement	
1	p	nonviolent	non-violence	
1	p	well	wellness	do good
2	p	empathetic	empathy	
2	p	good	goodness	
2	p	in good mood	good mood	
3	p	forgiven	forgiveness	forgive
4	p	capable	capacity	
4	p	confident	confidence	
4	p	different	difference	differentiate
4	p	friendly	friendship	
4	p	friendly	friendliness	
4	p	generous	generosity	
4	p	nude	nudity	go nude
4	p	obedient	obedience	obey
4	p	optimistic	optimism	
4	p	positive	positivism	
5	p	alive	life	live
5	p	bound	binding	bind
5	p	cool	cool	
5	p	delicate	delicacy	
5	p	determined	determination	determine
5	p	full of ardor	ardor	
5	p	full of energy	energy	energize
5	p	in control	control	

5	p	proud	pride	
5	p	useful	usefulness	
5	p	visionary	visionary	
6	p	carried away		carry away
6	p	enthused	enthusiasm	enthuse
6	p	enthusiastic	enthusiasm	
6	p	gentleman		
6	p	hot	heat	get warm
6	p	infatuated	infatuation	infatuate
6	p	mesmerized	mesmerization	mesmerize
7	p	agitated	agitation	agitate
7	p	amused	amusement	have fun
7	p	comic	comic	
7	p	energized	energy	energize
7	p	full of life	life	live
7	p	funny	fun	
7	p	have itchy feet	wanderlust	
7	p	having fun	fun	have fun
7	p	in laughter	laughter	laugh
7	p	laughing	laughter	laugh
7	p	mischievous		
7	p	strong	strength	
7	p	united	union	
8	p	admired	admiration	admired
8	p	attached	attachment	attach to
8	p	charmed	charm	charm
8	p	feel attachment from someone	attachment	
8	p	feel empathy for someone	empathy	
8	p	felt someone's affection	affection	
8	p	felt someone's sympathy	sympathy	
8	p	hopeful	hope	hope
8	p	intimate	intimacy	
8	p	loved	love	love
8	p	observed	observation	observe
8	p	sensitive	sensitivity	sensitize
8	p	stunned		stun
8	p	virile	virility	
8	p	vital	vitality	
8	p	watched		watch
8	p	women	femininity	
9	p	full of affection	affection	
9	p	full of hope	hope	

		adjective	name	verb
9	p	full of love	love	love
9	p	full of spirit	spirited	
9	p	full of warmth	warmth	
9	p	in love	love	love
9	p	love	love	love
9	p	lust in love	lust	fall in love
9	p	passionate	passion	
9	p	sentimental	feeling	feel
9	p	wondering	wonder	wonder
10	p	crazy	craziness	
10	p	emoted	emotion	emote
10	p	emotional	emotion	
10	p	emotive	emotion	
10	p	excited	excitation	excited
10	p	ignited		ignite myself
10	p	moved	emotion	be moved

rate s Surprise (doubt)

		adjective I feel	name I feel the	verb I
0	s	indifferent	indifference	
1	s	ambivalent	ambivalence	
1	s	emotionalized	emotionalism	emotionalize
1	s	hesitating	hesitation	hesitate
2	s	intrigued	intrigue	intrigue
2	s	of a reserve	reserve	
3	s	coaxed		coax
3	s	doubtful	doubt	doubt
3	s	in doubt	doubt	doubt
3	s	incredulous	incredulity	
3	s	mistrustful	mistrust	mistrust
3	s	skeptic	skepticism	
3	s	suspicious	hint	suspect
3	s	uncertain	uncertainty	
4	s	bad	badness	
4	s	confused	confusion	
4	s	destabilized		destabilize
4	s	disconcerting		disconcert
4	s	entangled		entangle
4	s	fussed	fuss	fuss

4	s	scrambled		scramble
4	s	tangled		tangle
4	s	uncomfortable		
4	s	unhorsed		unhorse
5	s	emoted	emotion	emote
5	s	emotional	emotion	
5	s	emotive	emotion	
5	s	entangled		entangle
5	s	moved	emotionality	move
6	s	stunned		stun
7	s	abashed	abashment	abash
7	s	crippled		cripple
7	s	disassembled		disassemble
7	s	dizzy	dizziness	make dizzy
7	s	embarrassed	embarrassment	embarrass
7	s	odd		
7	s	troubled	trouble	trouble
7	s	unstable	instability	destabilize
8	s	mesmerized	mesmerization	mesmerize
8	s	undermined		undermine
8	s	upset	upset	upset
9	s	hysterical	hysteria	
10	s	blocked	blockage	block
10	s	flabbergasted		flabbergast
10	s	in shock	shock	shock
10	s	stressed	stress	stress

Annex 3: The Structure of the seven types of information in Memory.

When we will build the EAI we will be able to know the contents of its memory in the same way that we can know the contents of a computer. This is among other things, what will allow us to verify the EAI's intentions, its personal values, long-term interests, if it has been corrupted, or infected with malicious information, etc.

When the brain decides on the emotion to feel, there are situations where the emotion is caused by a physical (or chemical) phenomenon and other times caused by the content of the information in memory.

In the first case, there are situations where the EAI will bump against an object, be knocked by a hammer, overheated by a fire, corroded by a chemical, etc. The senses observe physical (or chemical) harm and the brain records a pain, that is, only that there is a problem. Then the *Traumatism System* (**Table 10, Chapter 2**) gets activated using **"IF PAIN 1 THEN SURPRISE 1"** (**Chapters 2 and 4**) or for the EAI **"IF PROBLEM 1 THEN SURPRISE 1"**. This system searches its memory for an action to resolve the problem. It will be to the seven senses, that is, to each of the seven sensory machines, to deliver the information of pain thus only that there is a problem, nothing else. It's to the *Traumatism System*, all the senses and information contained in the memory to find a solution and an appropriate reaction. All these information will be stored in words in digital format as in a computer. Sometimes the EAI's sensor will deliver the word of the emotion. For example, the camera that identifies emotions on human's face (Shichuan et al., 2014), or the identification of chemicals, could transmit the signal indicating to the EAI to be afraid or not (e.g., fire, water, corrosive liquids or vapours). Similarly, if the EAI hears emotional expressions, it will be able to search its memory which contains the equivalent of the tables of **Annex 1** and **Annex 2** and find which of the seven fundamental emotions is expressed, as well as its intensity. It will then be able to react to this emotion.

Then there is the second situation, when the usual five senses do not provide us with emotional information, but the contents of memory and more accurately the *Lived experiences* (such as major *Traumatisms*) finds the emotion to feel. For example, if the EAI is afraid to parachute and another EAI does not have that fear. It depends on their previous experiences, the contents of their memory and the deductions they may do (the 6th and 7th senses). For these situations, the EAI's brain will find, like the human does, in its *Knowledge* and the whole the contents of its memory which emotion and intensity to live. Below is what the EAI's memory will contain. It will be very similar to that of a human, but probably in greater quantity.

The memory records what we lived as experiences using the seven senses. We do not yet know how the human's brain organizes the information it stores. In the artificial memory, we will use the existing technology to organize the collected information (which includes emotions, needs, *Knowledge*, personal *Values*, beliefs, *Traumatisms*, *Automatisms*, etc.). In a computer, we usually organize information in lists; or even better, in tables, similar to those we find in computer spreadsheets. The artificial memory will mainly contain seven tables as follows.

1) **A Table of personal *Lived experience*s**: A sequential list of our experiences which gives the history of our lives, year after year, day after day, hour after hour and, for the EAI, millisecond after millisecond. This table contains the videos of what we saw, the audios of what we have heard, as well as recordings of what we have tasted, smelled, felt by the external and internal touch, remembered from our memory and deducted. The recordings of the seven senses will therefore be linked to the place, day and time, the emotion felt (among the seven fundamental emotions) linked to the observation and the intensity of this emotion. We understand that for the human brain, there are times when some recordings are fuzzy or less accurate, some senses are fuzzy or less accurate, and some emotions are fuzzy or less accurate. The repetition of a recording can improve this fuzziness or not. *Each line of this table thus contains **five columns**: (i) a minimum of words identifying the observation (ii) the place (iii) time (iv) the recording from one of the seven senses, and (v) one of the seven fundamental emotions and its intensity X.* The description of the observation

is found in the Table of *Knowledge* below.

2) **A Table of *Traumatisms* and guilt experienced**: The brain contains a list of injuries and guilt experienced that mark psychologically, because fear was extreme, because the EAI believed he was about to break, or because he would not want to relive a mistake. The list contains the observation (video, audio, breakages experienced at different places due to impacts and felt by the sense of touch) and the intensity of the associated emotion. Even extreme, some are more extreme than others. We can live *Traumatisms* due to five emotions: fear, anger, guilt, distress and surprise. *Each line of this table contains **two columns**: (i) the observation, and (ii) the emotion and its intensity X.*

3) **A Table of *Valued information* and personal *Values* prioritized**: The brain contains a list of *Valued information,* personal values, principles, beliefs, prejudices, as well as personal preferences and interests of short, medium and long term. All these information are prioritized according to the importance that the EAI provide them for its protection, security, confidence and quality of life. *Each line of this table contains **two columns**: (i) the personal value, and (ii) the emotion and its intensity X.* The definitions related to the *Values* are found in the *Knowledge* table.

4) **A Table of prioritized *Knowledge***: This table contains in the first-place *Knowledge* that are currently important to us including those we have learned recently. These *Knowledge* are on top of the stack (at the top of the table), and are thus prioritized. Then comes our *Knowledge* that we often use, these days. Then there are all the other *Knowledge*. It's the linked emotion, the portion **"THEN PLEASURE of intensity X"** that prioritizes the Knowledge. The intensity X could vary from 1 to 10, 100 or 1000. *Each line of this table contains **three columns**: (i) the abbreviation for the concept (ii) the definition of the concept, and (iii) the fundamental emotion and its intensity X.* Definitions are often audio-videos. The emotion is usually **PLEASURE**, but a *Knowledge* may become dismissed (**ANGER**) because it ceases to please us. The abbreviation of the concept is important in the brain. For example, when using the terms "NASA," "U.N." or "blue helmets", these abbreviations allow us to summarize the concept and easily

understand using short and simple expressions. This allows to share more information in less time. In the table, we use the abbreviation to access the definition. When there is many "synonymous" abbreviations used, these are regrouped in the Table of *Groupings*, below. The definition is the understanding that the person or EAI makes about this concept in his brain. For each word, there may be one or more definitions: a short definition, an elaborated one, as well as one for each concept it may represent, as in a dictionary.

5) **A Table of *Groupings*, categorizations, synonyms, translations, acronyms and code simplification**: The brain contains groupings, categories, synonyms, translations, acronyms, classification codes, etc. Their definitions are found in the previous Table of *Knowledge*. For people who use multiple languages, the translation of a word is a synonym. *Each line of this table contains **three columns**: (i) the abbreviation of the concept (ii) a grouping or categorization, or a list of synonyms and translations, or a list of simplifications codes, as well as (iii) the emotion and its intensity X.*

6) **A Table of automatic reactions and *Automatisms***: For an athlete who repeats the same movements, the brain stores reactions that become automatic. Similarly, when we perform repetitive or routine work, we develop a method that becomes automatic. The EAI records a series of reactions no. 1, 2, 3, etc. according to each situation. *Each line of this table contains **three columns**: (i) the abbreviation for the event (ii) the suite of reactions that constitute the automatism, and (iii) the emotion and its intensity X.* The Table of *Knowledge* contains the event and the definitions related to the event.

7) **A dynamic Table of planned and prioritized *Interests***: It's the interests, needs and unfulfillments of the needs that the brain of the EAI feels and will activate. These interests are constantly changing (every millisecond). For example, if the robot throws a ball and fortuitously a dog jump on the robot during the throw, the robot will stop throwing to protect itself. The importance or intensity of the *Interests* (which are *Automatisms*) are known, and are hence prioritized. If the *Interest* is to throw the ball, the list of needs (take the ball, stretch the arms, move the arm back, then forward, then

release the ball from the fingers) are recorded on the first lines of the table. The current need (which is the priority) is always registered on the first line of the table (on top of the stack). This line No. 1 (taking the ball) activates the body. When the line is completed, it is erased and the second line (stretch the arm backwards) becomes the first line of the table, thus the priority that drives the body. Because the EAI like humans addresses several *Interests* simultaneously and accomplishes several *Interests* simultaneously - and also many tasks or actions simultaneously – the Table of *Interests* contains several sub-tables, one for each *Interest*. There is also a sub-table that prioritizes more or less all sub-tables. Each sub-table has a first line that powers a body part. Several lines No. 1 contain the action "waiting" (waiting for other activated priority interests to conclude). *Each line of this table contains **three columns**: (i) the abbreviation of an interest identifying also a sub-table (ii) the interest, need, solution, task, action or unfulfillment to satisfy a need, and (iii) a number indicating its importance in terms of priority.*

We note that all tables can be written in the format "**IF** an information **THEN** an emotion X" or "**IF** an info A **EQUALS** an info B **THEN** an emotion X" as explained in **Chapters 3 and 4** because they all contain two or three columns, except for the Table of *Experiences*, which can take the same form, by regrouping some columns. We also note that all the tables in the memory contain information regarding the emotions, and their intensities.

We realize here that the complexity of the behaviour of human beings lies not in the functioning of the emotions, nor the structure of the memory, which is generally the same for all of us, but in the massive amount of information that varies from one individual to the other.

We understand that there is no evidence that the memory of a human brain contains seven tables simply organized, but we can easily theorize that the human memory contains these seven types or lists of information. Talking about tables, lists or types of information inside the human memory is a clear, precise and useful way to understand each other.

Summary

- The memory of the EAI's artificial brain consists of seven tables:

1- Its personal *Lived experiences*,
2- Its experienced *Traumatisms* and guilts lived,
3- Its *Valued information* prioritized, or simply, its *Values*,
4- Its prioritized *Knowledge*,
5- Its *Groupings*, synonyms, translations, acronyms and abbreviations,
6- Its *Automatisms* and programmed reactions, and
7- Its *Interests* planned and prioritized to activate.

- The memory of the human brain contains probably the same seven sets of information.

- The Table of planned and prioritized *Interests* is dynamic and consists of multiple sub-tables that can be activated simultaneously.

About the Author

André Mainville was born in Montréal, Quebec, Canada, lived in Mont-St-Hilaire, has obtained a collegial diploma from C.E.G.E.P Maisonneuve, Montréal, a baccalaureate and master degrees from the Université Laval, Ste-Foy, Québec, in land surveying and geodesy, respectively; and then a doctorate degree from Ohio State University, Columbus, Ohio, U.S.A., in physical geodesy. He worked in cartography and geodesy for the Government of Canada, Ottawa, Ontario, modeling the gravitational field over Canada and managing large data bases. He is retired in Gatineau, Québec. It is his expertise and experience, acquired over a life time, in applied mathematics, computer programming, data management, sciences, scientific modeling and in management, as well as his interest in understanding human nature, that brought him at modeling an artificial intelligence. He his married, has three children and seven grand children.

www.ingramcontent.com/pod-product-compliance
Lightning Source LLC
Chambersburg PA
CBHW060022210326
41520CB00009B/971